Wounds That Heal

BRINGING OUR HURTS TO THE CROSS

STEPHEN SEAMANDS

InterVarsity Press
Downers Grove, Illinois

InterVarsity Press
P.O. Box 1400, Downers Grove, IL 60515-1426
World Wide Web: www.ivpress.com
E-mail: mail@ivpress.com

InterVarsity Press® is the book-publishing division of InterVarsity Christian Fellowship/USA®, a student
movement active on campus at hundreds of universities, colleges and schools of nursing in the United States
of America, and a member movement of the International Fellowship of Evangelical Students. For information
about local and regional activities, write Public Relations Dept., InterVarsity Christian Fellowship/USA, 6400
Schroeder Rd., P.O. Box 7895, Madison, WI 53707-7895, or visit the IVCF website at <www.ivcf.org>.

Scripture quotations, unless otherwise noted, are from the New Revised Standard Version of the Bible,
copyright 1989 by the Division of Christian Education of the National Council of the Churches of Christ in
the USA. Used by permission. All rights reserved.

While all of the stories and examples in this book come from real people and events, some names and
identifying details have been altered to protect the privacy of the individuals involved.

"The Stripes I Wear" is used by permission.
Pages 83-84 from The Lion, the Witch and the Wardrobe by C. S. Lewis copyright © C. S. Lewis Pte. Ltd.
1950. Extract reprinted by permission.
The song "At the Cross" by Randy and Terry Butler on pages 12-13 ©1993 Mercy/Vineyard Publishing
(ASCAP) is used by permission. All rights reserved.

Every effort has been made to trace and contact copyright holders for additional materials quoted in this book.
The author will be pleased to rectify any omissions in future editions if notified by copyright holders.

Cover design: Cindy Kiple
Cover and interior image: Digital Vision/Getty Images
ISBN 0-8308-3225-4

Printed in the United States of America ∞

Library of Congress Cataloging-in-Publication Data

Seamands, Stephen A., 1949-
  Wounds that heal: bringing our hurts to the cross/Stephen
  Seamands
     p. cm.
Includes bibliographical references.
  ISBN 0-8308-3225-4 (pbk.: alk paper)
  1. Pastoral theology—Biblical teaching. 2. Jesus
Christ—Crucifixion—Biblical teaching. 3. Bible. N.T.—Criticism,
interpretation, etc. I. Title.
  BS2545.P45S43 2003
  232'.3—dc21
                                                                    2003006844

| P | 17 | 16 | 15 | 14 | 13 | 12 | 11 | 10 | 9 | 8 | 7 | 6 | 5 | 4 | 3 |
| Y | 15 | 14 | 13 | 12 | 11 | 10 | 09 | 08 | 07 | 06 | 05 | 04 |

To Carol

She is far more precious than jewels.

The heart of her husband trusts in her,

and he will have no lack of gain.

She does him good, and not harm,

all the days of her life. (Proverbs 31:10-12)

Contents

Contents

1

Bringing Our Hurts to the Cross

Think not thou canst sigh a sigh
And thy Maker is not by;
Think not thou canst weep a tear
And thy Maker is not near.
O! He gives to us His joy
That our griefs He may destroy;
Till our grief is fled and gone
He doth sit by us and moan.

WILLIAM BLAKE

The movie *Forrest Gump* contains a heartwrenching scene where five-year-old Jenny, Forrest's friend, prays as the two of them are running into a cornfield to hide from her drunken father: "Dear God, make me a bird so I can fly far, far away from here."

Her father had been sexually abusing her, and although the next day he was arrested and Jenny went to live with someone else, her struggles over what he did to her had only begun. In fact, she spends the rest of her life trying to recover from the damage.

Years later, Jenny returns to the small town where she grew up to visit Forrest. The two of them, now adults in their thirties, are walking near the abandoned shack where she once lived. As she fixes her eyes on it, painful buried memories of the abuse flood her mind.

She bursts into tears and begins to vent her hurt and anger by picking up the rocks around her and throwing them as hard as she can at the shack. When there are no more rocks, she takes off her shoes and throws them too. Finally, she falls to the ground sobbing.

As Forrest reflects on the scene he says, "Sometimes I guess there just *aren't* enough rocks."

As you consider the hurt and pain in your life, do you find yourself resonating with what Forrest said? Perhaps you were verbally, physically or sexually abused, experienced the wrenching pain of a divorce, grew up in a chaotic home with an alcoholic parent, or lost a loved one in a senseless accident. Maybe you have been deeply hurt in a relationship or have felt the aching loneliness of abandonment. Were you born with a physical handicap or ridiculed as a child by siblings and other children? Could it be that you were treated unfairly in a work situation or betrayed by people in your church?

Like Jenny, deep-seated pain and anger may still fester in your heart. At times you may find yourself shaking a clenched fist toward heaven as a raging voice within cries out, *God, it isn't fair! It's not right. What did I do to deserve this?* We agree with Forrest Gump: "Sometimes there just *aren't* enough rocks."

COME TO THE CROSS

Over the years, as bruised and broken people have shared their wrenching stories with me, the inner voice of the Spirit has prompted me to offer them a special invitation: "Come with me. Come with me to Calvary. Come stand beneath the cross of Jesus. Gaze with me at the twisted, tortured figure hanging there. Consider the broken, bleeding Son of God. Reflect on *your* hurts and wounds in the light of *his*."

During eleven years as a pastor, I frequently preached about the cross. When I was a doctoral student in theology, I chose the doctrine of the atonement for one of my comprehensive exams. As a seminary professor of Christian doctrine since 1983, I have taught about the cross every semester in classes such as "Basic Christian Theology" and "The Person and Work of Christ." So I have had a lifelong interest in the cross of Christ.

But in the early 1990s, as a result of several personal experiences and my growing involvement in what I can best describe as a ministry of healing prayer to persons with emotional and spiritual needs, I began to witness firsthand the power of the cross in ways I had never imagined. As I have counseled and prayed with people, and together we have surveyed the wondrous cross, I have been stunned and awed by its power to heal painful hurts. Isaiah was surely right: by his wounds we *are* healed (Isaiah 53:5). His nail-scarred hands truly are able to bind up the brokenhearted and loose the chains of those who are bound.

Although I have written from the perspective of a pastoral theologian, not that of a counselor, my prayer is that if you are a person who needs to experience emotional and spiritual healing, this book will help you bring your hurts to the foot of the cross. If you are a professional Christian counselor, pastor, lay counselor or someone who engages in a ministry of healing prayer, I also pray it will further equip you so that you can bring your clients or those to whom you minister to the cross. Finally, if you are a believer desiring to grow in your understanding of the cross or an inquirer seeking to learn about the Christian faith, I pray that considering the cross and its relation to human hurts will cause you to grasp its wonder-working power as never before.

Make no mistake. Bringing our hurts to the cross is not simply praying a few bold prayers for healing that will automatically solve everything. The cross demonstrates that for the complex problem of evil and suffering there is no simplistic, quick-fix method of restoration and healing—even for God.

Jesus' crucified body was resurrected and glorified, but he still

bore the scars from his wounds. In fact, they have become his identifying marks (John 20:20-29). Songwriter Michael Card says Jesus is
"known by the scars." And it will always be that way. His scars are permanent—they are eternal scars. When the apostle John looked in
his heavenly vision to see who would open the sealed scroll revealing
the final course of history, he saw "a Lamb standing as if it had been
slaughtered" (Revelation 5:6). Such was the price that Jesus, the
Lamb of God (John 1:29), paid and the long-term commitment that
God made for our restoration and healing.

Bringing our hurts to the cross, then, is not a quick-fix method of
healing. Deep wounds require deep healing. And deep healing involves a slow and difficult process. Like peeling an onion, it generally happens one tearful layer at a time. The process may be punc-
tuated with major breakthroughs; nonetheless, it is long and
arduous. Three steps forward are sometimes followed by two steps
backward. It requires courage and determination—often more than
we alone can muster. Without the encouragement and strength
Jesus imparts to us, we would be unable to finish the journey.

Still, there is nothing more therapeutic than bringing our hurts to
the cross of Christ. The cross illumines our hurts. It sheds light on
them. It gives us a different perspective from which to view them.
Reframed with wood from Calvary's cross, our painful memory pictures look different.

But the cross not only illumines our hurts, it also heals and transforms them as expressed in "At the Cross," a beautiful praise song
written by Randy and Terry Butler:

> I know a place, a wonderful place
> Where accused and condemned
> Find mercy and grace
> Where the wrongs we have done
> And the wrongs done to us

> Were nailed there with him
> There on the cross
>
> At the cross (At the cross)
> He died for our sin
> At the cross (At the cross)
> He gave us life again[1]

How wonderfully true! The cross is "a place, a wonderful place" where there is "mercy and grace" for those who have been "accused and condemned" and deeply wounded. What healing grace and power there is in his nail-scarred hands! At the cross he ministers to our wounds by touching them with his.

On the one hand, bringing our hurts and wounds to the cross is quite simple. As hymn writer Fanny Crosby puts it, "Free to all, a healing stream, Flows from Calv'ry's mountain." And as the praise song says, the cross is "where accused and condemned find mercy and grace." It is the place of forgiveness and healing, deliverance and freedom, mercy and grace. By his wounds we are healed.

On the other hand, bringing our hurts to the cross is complex. In reaction to our wounds, we have erected protective structures to avoid dealing with them or allowing anyone to touch them. We have believed lies that God doesn't care—at least, not about us—and doesn't want to heal our wounds. Resentment and bitterness toward our offenders may be simmering in our hearts. Unhealthy responses and destructive habits precipitated by our emotional pain have become comfortable. To come to the cross, we must confront and deal with these issues.

To bring our wounds to the foot of the cross, we have to walk the road to the cross and choose the way of the cross. As we shall discover, this means choosing the way of acceptance rather than denial, confronting instead of concealing. It also means choosing costly forgiveness over resentment and bearing unjust suffering over retaliation.

The road we must travel is indeed less traveled—a rough, risky road, not a smooth, safe superhighway. To step onto that road is one thing; to walk that road until we arrive at the foot of the cross is another. Sometimes after our first flush of enthusiasm for the journey, we want to turn back. The road appears too rugged, the goal too distant. The ascent up the hill called Mount Calvary is steeper than we imagined, the effort more costly.

Often we will falter, but as we patiently press on we make a joyful discovery: not only is there mercy and grace when we finally get to the cross, it is there all along the way. From the moment we take our first step on that road to the moment we experience deep healing at the foot of the cross, we are never alone. Jesus walks before us, leading the way. Step into any dark, unknown place—his nail-scarred footprints are already there. Better still, Jesus walks alongside us, encouraging our spirits. The further we journey, the more we discover the depth of his affection and tenderness toward us. Jesus also walks behind us holding us up when our knees wobble. We can lean on him, for his strength is perfectly tailored to our weaknesses. And because God's mercy and grace accompany us, we receive courage and determination to stay on the road and continue the journey.

A MAN OF SORROWS AND FAMILIAR WITH SUFFERING

What is involved in bringing our hurts to the cross? What are the stopping points along the way, the stations along the Via Dolorosa? And why is the cross such a powerful instrument for healing?

In the chapters that follow, we will explore those questions in detail, particularly in relation to emotional healing. With our zoom lens, in chapters two through six, we will narrow and intensify our focus to see how the cross addresses destructive effects of human hurts such as rejection, shame, disappointment with God, addictions and demonization. Then in chapters seven through ten, we will consider what the cross tells us about how healing happens, as we think about embracing our pain, forgiving those who have wronged us, loving our enemies and offering our wounds to God.

But in the rest of this chapter, let's put emotional suffering in a broader context. Using a wide-angle lens, we want to consider how the cross addresses human suffering in general, especially the problem it raises for faith in God.

From the ancient book of Job to Rabbi Harold Kushner's recent bestseller *When Bad Things Happen to Good People*, people everywhere have wrestled with how an all-powerful and all-loving God can allow so much suffering—especially unjust suffering—to exist in the world.

In Dostoyevsky's great novel *The Brothers Karamazov*, the child of a poor Russian serf, while playing one day, accidentally hits one of his master's prize hunting dogs with a stone. When he finds out about it, the master is enraged. He has the boy seized and, turning his vicious dogs loose, forces the boy's mother to watch as they tear her son to pieces.

> When Ivan, one of the main characters in the story, hears about what the master has done, he shakes his head in disbelief. Then after a long reflection on how a good and righteous God could possibly allow such a thing to happen, he concludes, "It's not God that I cannot accept. . . . I accept God, understand that, but I cannot accept the world that He has made."[2]

We too echo Ivan's bewilderment as we confront the cruelty of such unjust suffering. Disturbing, perplexing thoughts arise in our minds, creating unwanted challenges to our faith.

How does the cross shed light on this critical problem? How can it speak to us as we struggle to believe in God's power and goodness in the face of unjust suffering? In no uncertain terms, the cross tells us that God in Christ is one with us in our suffering. When we suffer, God doesn't stand off, aloof and unconcerned, unable or unwilling to get involved. Jesus, the Eternal Word of God, has "become flesh and lived among us" (John 1:14). He is Emmanuel, which means God with us (Matthew 1:23); and at the cross, the depth of his involvement with us is fully revealed.

On the cross, Jesus personally experienced the full range of human suffering. Pastoral theologian Frank Lake puts it like this: "It is an astonishing fact that the events of the Crucifixion of Jesus Christ portray every variety of human suffering and evil."[3] He points out that on the cross Jesus suffered injustice, felt the shame of nakedness, was deprived of his rights, endured taunting, was the focus of others' rage, and was rejected and forsaken. He also endured excruciating physical pain, thirst, hunger, emptiness, torment, confusion and finally, death itself. Lake expresses it so beautifully:

> Christ's own being on the Cross contained all the clashing contrarities and scandalous fates of human existence. Life Himself was identified with death; the Light of the world was enveloped in darkness. The feet of the Man who said, "I am the Way" feared to tread upon it and prayed, "If it be possible, not that way." The Water of Life was thirsty. The Bread of Life was hungry. The divine Lawgiver was Himself unjustly outlawed. The Holy One was identified with the unholy. The Lion of Judah was crucified as a lamb. The hands that made the world and raised the dead were fixed by nails until they were rigid in death. Men's hope of heaven descended into hell.[4]

This means Jesus can truly identify with us when we suffer because he has personally experienced the breadth and the depth of human suffering. In the New Testament book of Hebrews we read that he is a faithful high priest because he "learned obedience through what he suffered" (5:8) and was made "perfect through sufferings"(2:10). Because he has been "touched with the feelings of our infirmities" (4:15 KJV), he can empathetically identify with our distress.

But not only did Jesus suffer personally on the cross; he also suffered vicariously. In the words of the Old Testament prophet Isaiah, he is not only "a man of sorrows and acquainted with grief" but "surely he has borne *our* griefs, and carried *our* sorrows" (53:4 NKJV, emphasis added). In his classic commentary, Franz Delitzsch states that in this verse "the meaning is not merely that the Servant of God entered into the fellowship of our sufferings, but that He took upon Himself the sufferings which we had to bear and deserved to bear, and therefore not only took them away . . . but bore them in His own person, that He might deliver us from them."[5] On the cross, then, Jesus bore not only his own suffering but, in some mysterious way, yours, mine and the suffering of the whole world as well. As Karl Stern, the eminent Jewish psychiatrist who saw friends and family dragged away to torture and death in Nazi concentration camps, and who converted to Christianity after World War II, expresses so forcefully:

> There is something extraordinary in the suffering of Christ. It seems to include all human suffering. . . . The more you dwell on it, the more it becomes clear that in His agony He anticipated the hidden agonies of innumerable individuals. . . . It anticipates, it contains your life and my life in a singular way.[6]

When we first heard the good news of salvation, most of us were likely told that Christ died for our sins. In Isaiah's unforgettable words, "He was wounded for our transgressions, he was bruised for our iniquities" and "the Lord has laid on him the iniquity of us all"(Isaiah 53:5-6 NKJV). Scripture underscores this wonderful truth again and again. As Peter puts it, "He himself bore our sins in his body on the cross" (1 Peter 2:24).

However, we also need to stress that on the cross he bore our sufferings as well. The bad news is that we are both sinners and sufferers, villains and victims; the good news is that the cross addresses

both conditions. The writers of the praise song quoted earlier rightly
grasp this. Notice that both

The wrongs we have done [sinners]
And the wrongs done to us [sufferers]
Were nailed there with him
There on the cross.

This means that Christ not only identifies with us completely in
our suffering because he has had an experience like ours, he also
participates in our suffering because our very own experience of suffering has mysteriously been laid upon him.

Several days after I had explained this truth to a woman who as a
child had been subjected to ritual acts of sexual abuse by a group of
men, she sent me an e-mail describing its powerful impact on her:

I keep turning your thought over and over in my mind—that
Jesus wasn't just there, he experienced the same abuse and degradation I did. . . . The men who used me in their rituals were
not just engaged in ordinary, run-of-the-mill evil, focused on
just the victim and their own gratification; instead, they were
actively working against the Lord of Light and Life, and they
knew that's what they were doing . . . yet Christ chose to experience those things anyway, all for my sake. The idea is so enor-
mous, so incredible, I know I haven't begun to take it in. Yes,
he died for me, and that was his ultimate gift, but somehow this
hits far closer to home. . . . Jesus was there, and Jesus experienced it all. He didn't just watch, and say, "There, there," or
even "I love you." Jesus experienced it all.

But not only did Jesus experience it all, bearing our suffering as
he hung on the cross; God the Father, through his Son, experienced
it too. George Buttrick, a great twentieth-century preacher, tells
about a painting of the crucifixion that hangs in an Italian church.

At first glance, it appears to be like most paintings of the crucifixion, but on closer examination, one perceives that "there's a vast and shadowy figure behind the figure of Jesus. The nail that pierces the hand of Jesus goes through the hand of God. The spear thrust into the side of Jesus goes through into God's."[7] As the apostle Paul says, "God was in Christ reconciling the world to himself"(2 Corinthians 5:19 NKJV).

THE MAN OF SORROWS IS ENOUGH

Of course, knowing that God suffers with us doesn't make our pain disappear or explain the enigma of suffering, but it does enable us to keep trusting God and believing in his goodness, even in the midst of the inexplicable. We may not be able to trace God's hand in what has happened, but we can still trust God's heart. And trusting God's heart encourages us to turn toward him, instead of away from him, to turn toward the cross and the road we must travel to get there.

Joni Eareckson Tada reached this conclusion as she reflected on her own life as a quadriplegic and the lives of countless others who suffer a similar plight. An athletic teenager, Joni was paralyzed in a diving accident in Chesapeake Bay in 1967. Putting her life together after the accident seemed impossible, and at times she sank into total despair, furious that God had allowed this to happen to her. For Joni, the slow change from bitterness back to trust in God dragged out over three years of tears and violent questions. But through her determination and the support of family and friends, she finally came to believe that God loved her and had not abandoned her.

For the past thirty years Joni has ministered far and wide. Through her books, public speaking and work on behalf of the disabled, along with her unique mouth paintings (she holds the brush between her teeth!), God has used her to touch scores of people. As a result, she receives thousands of letters and, not surprisingly, the majority revolve around the problem of suffering. Joni doesn't pretend to have all the answers, but she believes that knowing Jesus suffered is the greatest key to enduring our suffering and finding healing for our wounds. She says:

> When you are hurting, when your heart is being wrung out like a sponge, when you've just become a quadriplegic, when your husband has just left you, when your son has committed suicide, to try to come up with answers is pointless. . . . The only answer that satisfies is to think of that greater affliction—Christ on the cross. And one day he will give us the key that will unlock sense out of it all. But until then, the Man of Sorrows is enough.[8]

Yes, the Man of Sorrows is enough—enough to cause us, even in the face of our affliction, to ultimately turn not away but toward God and the road that leads to the cross.

Dennis Ngien, an international evangelist and pastor in Canada, tells about a conversation he had with a Czech government official as he was returning home on a plane following a preaching tour in the former Czechoslovakia. The man had attended one of the services where Ngien had preached about Christ's suffering for his people. However, instead of inspiring him to trust in God, he left the service cursing God, his mind swirling around the forty years of torment he and his family had experienced during Communist rule, particularly his parents' death by starvation and his own wrenching experience growing up in an orphanage.

When the man arrived home, he continued to burn with rage. His eyes fell on a crucifix hanging on his apartment wall that his mother had given him before she died. She had prayed that someday he would come to know Christ, but seeing it fueled his anger even more. He was so upset that he picked up a cake topped with thick white icing and threw it at the crucifix. The cake hit the crucifix and the icing clung to it. Then it slowly began to drip off the face of the crucified Jesus hanging there.

At that very moment Ngien's words about Christ's suffering resounded in his mind. As he stared intently at the figure of Jesus, he noticed there were tears in his eyes. He was so moved by them that he fell on his knees before the cross and surrendered his life to Christ. "Christ is for me, not against me," he exclaimed.

"I don't understand many of the things that happened politically," the man told Ngien as they continued to talk on the plane, "but I know that Jesus did not forsake me. He was in pain when I was in pain. He was in tears when I was in tears. He did not experience joy when I suffered most."[9]

Ngien, reflecting on the Czech official's words, comments: "Forgoing speculation as to why suffering befell him, he was now risking himself to the loving care of the Divine Sufferer. It sufficed this wounded governor to perceive in the Cross God's deepest pain and his loving scars."[10]

Like Jenny throwing rocks or the Czech government official throwing cake, we may find ourselves throwing things as we confront the intense pain of our undeserved hurts. After all, the road to the cross is strewn with rocks and other objects thrown by rage-filled sufferers down through the centuries.

So Christ's invitation to us still stands: "Come, walk this rugged road with me. Throw rocks if you have to. But don't turn away—turn toward the cross. Ponder your affliction in the light of my greater affliction; consider your wounds in the light of mine."

QUESTIONS FOR PERSONAL OR GROUP REFLECTION

1. In what life situation have you most identified with Jenny from *Forrest Gump* as she throws rocks and shoes at her childhood home?

2. If the suffering of Christ could speak with words to your own suf-

fering, what would it say? How does reflection on his agony affect you? How does your agony affect him?

3. When we seek to come to the cross with our pain, we may encounter numerous obstacles: protective structures, lies, resentments, bitterness, unhealthy responses to our emotional pain and destructive habits. What specifically has kept you from coming to the cross with your pain? Are you willing to bring these obstacles to the foot of the cross, asking Jesus to remove them?

4. To walk in the way of the cross, we must embrace new and healthier habits of the heart, "acceptance rather than denial, confronting instead of concealing, . . . choosing costly forgiveness over resentment and bearing unjust suffering over retaliation." What might walking the way of the cross mean for us?

5. "Christ not only identifies with us completely in our suffering because he has had an experience like ours, he also participates in our suffering because our very own experience of suffering has mysteriously been laid upon him" (p. 18). Reflect on the meaning of this for yourself and for people in general.

6. Was there an important time when you didn't trust God's heart, when you ran away from him rather than toward him? How does a greater understanding of Jesus' suffering enable you to run toward him without reservation?

Part One

THE CROSS AND THE

DAMAGING EFFECTS

OF HUMAN HURTS

2

Despised and Rejected

Children descend into hell when love is squeezed out of them by parental neglect. There is a connection between this and the rejection of Christ.

FRANK LAKE

Rejection. We have all felt the pain and sting of it. "To discard or throw out as worthless, useless, or substandard; cast off or out"[1]— that's one dictionary's definition of *rejection*. But it doesn't begin to convey the intense anguish, the agony rejection inflicts on the human spirit. Deep-seated feelings of rejection are at the core of many human hurts. So in bringing our wounds to the cross, our experience of rejection is a good place to begin.

THE MANY FACES OF REJECTION

Of course, rejection wears multiple faces; it comes in a variety of shapes and sizes. Sometimes we experience it as a direct frontal assault on our humanity—like being run over by a freight train.

The MTV series *The Real World* presents the real-life happenings of seven twentysomethings from various backgrounds who live together in the same house. In one episode, a young woman told two of her male housemates about a letter she wrote when she was eight years old to a father she had never known because of divorce. "I just want you to know about me," the letter said. "I like hopscotch, biology, and dissecting things. You don't have to respond, but I just wanted you to know about your daughter."

Her letter came back unopened with these words scrawled across the envelope: "Return to sender—send no more letters!"

Tearfully she described to her friends the impact of her father's rejection: "Ever since then I've sought acceptance from men through boyfriends. I hate it! I'm a feminist, and I still have this need to have acceptance from men."

Parents deal out pain in a variety of ways, and children remember their words forever:

- "If I were a good mother, I would have put you in a foster home by now."

- "If you tell anyone [about the sexual abuse], I'll kill you. And don't think anyone will care if you do. It's part of growing up and you'd better get used to it."

- "You were an accident, a mistake. We never wanted you and we never will."

- "If there's a wrong way to do something, you'll find it."

- "You were supposed to have been a boy."

- "You're as useless as a wart on a pickle."

Words like these cut to the heart's core. Sticks and stones can't compare to the harm they inflict.

Sometimes rejection may not be so blatant and direct, yet its effects are just as devastating. At the seminary where I teach, a student in his mid-thirties came to see me for counsel and prayer. The stress of being a pastor, student, husband and father was more than he could handle. He was coming unglued, and in several recent situations his volcanic anger had erupted. To escape his frustration he found himself turning to Internet pornography.

External pressure was stirring up unresolved childhood pain. I explained it to him like this: "When you squeeze a tube of toothpaste, it makes the toothpaste inside the tube come out. That's what's happening to you. The outside pressure is causing what's inside you to come to the surface."

As we began to talk about his growing up years, he described his relationship with his father: "All my life I've loved football. I played all the time when I was a kid. I played in junior high. I was a star linebacker in high school. I got a scholarship to play football in college. After college, I even played semi-pro football for awhile.

"My father is not a mean man. He would never say or do anything to intentionally hurt you. But my father is a workaholic. He wasn't ever around when I was growing up. And he has never once in my life seen me play football."

He spoke those words matter-of-factly, but they stunned me. Football was an activity he enjoyed and excelled at. Yet his father, whose acceptance and affirmation he—like every child—needed so desperately, was *never* there to watch him and cheer him on. In that moment, my heart ached for him. "I'm *so* sorry," I said, "so sorry."

My sympathetic response caught him off guard and made him uncomfortable. He was silent, but the look on his face said, "Why are you making such a big deal about this?"

Because it *was* a big deal. According to Frank Lake, "Children descend into hell when love is squeezed out of them by parental neglect."[2] The student's unwillingness to own his soul wound of rejection was his way of protecting himself from anguish and keeping a lid on his anger toward his father.

Rejection can be experienced in even subtler ways. Leanne Payne tells about a time when she was attending a conference on healing prayer for ministers, counselors and health-care professionals.[3] During one of the sessions, while the leader was praying for the unhealed hurts of those at the conference, the Holy Spirit whispered to her, "Forgive your father for dying."

Her father had died when she was three years old. It had never occurred to her that she had interpreted his death as a personal rejection. *How ridiculous,* she thought, *to forgive one's father for dying.* But the Spirit's voice intensified. Finally, in obedience, she forgave her father.

As a result, Christ came and healed the deep hurt of that unknown rejection. Pain that she had carried for years finally left her. From that point on, Leanne could relate more comfortably to men. A disturbing recurring dream ceased, one in which she anxiously searched for her father and eventually found his casket, meanwhile hoping against hope he was still alive.

Like Leanne, we too may unknowingly have interpreted losses in our lives as personal rejection. In *The Primal Wound,*[4] Nancy Verrier maintains that no matter how early or smoothly adoption occurs, *every* adopted child interprets being separated from its biological mother as personal rejection. Children of divorce generally perceive the split up of their parents as rejection too.

WHY REJECTION WOUNDS SO DEEPLY

To understand why rejection wounds so deeply, we must grasp an essential fact about human personhood. As Christians, our starting point in understanding persons is our belief that human beings have been created in the image of God (Genesis 1:26-27). True human personhood is thus patterned after divine personhood.

Our understanding of divine personhood is grounded in the belief that God is *one* but exists in the communion of *three* persons: Father, Son and Holy Spirit. Moreover, when we consider the three persons of the triune God, we understand the uniqueness of each not by accentuating their separateness from one another but by focusing on their relationships with one another. Their very names—

Father, Son, Holy Spirit—imply they exist in relationship with one another. The Father is known as Father by virtue of his relationship to the Son and vice versa. The Spirit is Spirit by virtue of interaction with the other two.

Taking our cue from divine personhood, we conclude that persons exist not separate from, but in relationship with, others. This understanding challenges the Western individualistic way of thinking where persons are primarily separate selves, free to act on their own. Western individualism says, "I am myself as I stand apart from you." According to the Christian view, "I am myself as I stand in relationship to you."

Relationships, then, are essential to human personhood. We cannot be persons apart from our connection to others. This explains why wounds of rejection cut so deeply, particularly those wounds inflicted during our early years when our sense of personhood is being formed. Rejection strikes a blow at the root of healthy human personhood because it strikes at our connection to others. When a parent rejects a child, the child hears the parent saying, "I don't want a relationship with you." But as children, we desperately need to relate to our parents. Our very personhood, our sense of being, depends on it.

Unconditional acceptance and affirmation from parents are so vital and necessary. Without these relational foundation stones, these ties that bind and bond us to them, a proper sense of self will not develop. Remove them completely, and we will exist at the subpersonal level of nonbeing.

Acceptance and affirmation from others are also foundational in developing a proper self-love. As significant others accept and affirm us, we grow to affirm and accept ourselves. If they believe we are lovable and enjoyable, we can believe it too. But when we are rejected by others, we learn to reject ourselves. Frank Lake poignantly describes how babies and infants who experience severe and prolonged rejection by parents are left with a feeling of inner badness.

It is a bad thing that I am here at all. I am synonymous with bad relationships. As for trying to create relationships with others, this would only be to infect them with my badness. If, by some strange force of threatening love, a poor fool falls in love with me, I can only show my love and care paradoxically by driving him or her away. I am nothing. If people expect to receive love from me, they will be horribly mistaken. I cannot bear anyone to look inside me, or come close enough to see that the cupboard of my soul is wretchedly bare.[5]

Such rejection creates a devastating effect. One woman, whose alcoholic mother constantly called her names like "b——" and told her she was going to hell, described how such verbal abuse shaped her view of herself: "I could never understand what I had done to make my mother hate me so much. I certainly couldn't be lovable. I saw myself as a complete waste of life."

Which of your experiences of rejection have wounded you deeply? How have they affected your view of yourself? Have they fueled self-contempt and self-hatred? You may not have experienced the deep-level rejection of those we have described, yet even when not as deep, rejection can cut to the core of our being and produce deadly fruit. Leanne Payne is right: "Unhealed rejections become seedbeds of diseased 'matter' such as bitterness, envy, rage, fear of rejection, and a sense of inferiority."[6]

HE WAS DESPISED AND REJECTED

Just as we are wounded by rejection, Christ also suffered rejection. When we consider our affliction in light of the indescribable rejection he endured on the cross, our perspective begins to change.

He was despised and rejected by others . . .
and as one from whom others hide their faces
he was despised, and we held him of no account. (Isaiah 53:3)

Written several hundred years before Christ's death, Isaiah's incredibly accurate description of the Suffering Servant sums up what Jesus experienced. Henri Blocher, in reflecting on Isaiah's words, says, "The need for acceptance, esteem, acknowledgment, is one of the basic hungers of human personality, especially of such a sensitive and open personality as the Servant's. How agonizing to be starved of them! The Servant will be utterly despised by men."[7]

Jesus knew the sting of rejection throughout his life. He was born in a smelly stable, forced to flee the country, treated with contempt by the religious establishment, spurned in his hometown and even misunderstood by his family. In the prologue of his Gospel, John sums up it up well: "He came to what was his own, and his own people did not accept him" (John 1:11). But all the rejection came to an excruciating climax on Good Friday.

The rejection of neglect. During his last meal with his disciples, Jesus' heart was heavy. John writes that he was "troubled in spirit" (John 13:21) as he told them that one of them, his closest friends, would betray him. But during the entire meal the disciples seemed oblivious about what was unfolding and insensitive to what Jesus was feeling. As usual, they were totally preoccupied with themselves, engaging in debates as to which one of them was the greatest (Luke 22:24-27).

When they left the upper room and went to the Garden of Gethsemane, their disregard for Jesus' needs was even more conspicuous. Over supper they had failed to notice Jesus was deeply troubled. How could they miss it now when he explicitly said, "I am deeply grieved, even to death." He even pleaded, "Remain here, and stay awake with me"(Matthew 26:38). Jesus desperately needed their support, but all they could do was snore.

The sting of neglect. Close friends who promise to be faithful but are so preoccupied with themselves, they fail you when you need them most. Jesus knew exactly what such neglectful rejection felt like.

The rejection of disloyalty. For three years he had loved his disciples and poured himself into them. Despite all their failures and foolishness, he believed in them. He had never been disloyal.

Of course, they too swore they would always be loyal. That fateful night when Jesus predicted, "You will all become deserters," Peter reacted vehemently: "Even though I must die with you, I will not deny you." All the others also declared their undying loyalty (Mark 14:27-31).

But within a few hours, Jesus' prediction came true. When the shepherd was struck, all the sheep scattered. "Jesus who?" exclaimed Peter twice when a servant girl insisted he was one of Christ's disciples. And the third time, as others chimed in with her, he took an oath: "I swear, I have no idea who you're talking about"(see Mark 14:66-72).

Jesus knew the rejection that overwhelms you when those who are bound to you treat you like a stranger. According to Luke's account, immediately after his third denial "the Lord turned and looked at Peter" (Luke 22:61). Can you imagine the expression on Jesus' face? Perhaps there were tears in his eyes.

The rejection of betrayal. Treating people to whom you are bound as if they were *strangers* is unforgivable; turning against them as if they were *enemies* is unconscionable. Jesus experienced this betrayal—perhaps the most terrible form of personal rejection. Judas, one of the trusted twelve, betrayed him with a kiss, a sign of intimacy and affection, as he handed Jesus over to the soldiers who had come to arrest him.

Centuries earlier, in the same vicinity where Jesus was betrayed, his ancestor King David had a similar experience. David was fleeing from his palace in Jerusalem to escape from his own son Absalom, who was leading an insurrection. So "David went up the ascent of the Mount of Olives, weeping as he went" (2 Samuel 15:30). Then, to make matters worse, he learned that Ahithophel, his longtime friend and trusted advisor, "was among the conspirators with Absalom" (2 Samuel 15:31).

David composed Psalm 55 after experiencing the betrayal of a close friend, possibly Ahithophel. Eugene Peterson's paraphrase of that psalm catches what David was feeling:

My insides are turned inside out;
    Specters of death have me down.
I shake with fear,
    I shudder from head to foot. . . .

This isn't the neighborhood bully
    mocking me—I could take that.
This isn't a foreign devil spitting
    invective—I could tune that out.
It's *you!* We grew up together!
    You! My best friend!
Those long hours of leisure as we walked
    arm in arm, God a third party to our conversation. . . .

And this, my best friend, betrayed his best friends;
    his life betrayed his word.
All my life I've been charmed by his speech,
    never dreaming he'd turn on me.
His words, which were music to my ears,
    turned to daggers in my heart.

(Psalm 55:4-5, 12-14, 20-21 The Message)

Like David, Jesus experienced such daggers too. He knew the rejection of being stabbed in the back by those closest to him, wounded in the house of his friends (Zechariah 13:6).

The rejection of unfairness. Jesus was innocent. None of his interrogators—Caiaphas, Herod, even Pilate—could find any fault with him. Indeed, they were the ones guilty of gross injustice. The Jewish law prescribed the procedure they should have followed: first a trial, and if the defendant was found guilty, then condemnation and punishment. As it turned out, Jesus never really had a formal trial.

The religious leaders decided beforehand that he needed to be eliminated. After his arrest they interrogated him, but all along they knew he had to die. Even if he had been guilty of blasphemy—the main charge leveled against him—the punishment should have been death by stoning, not crucifixion. However, crucifixion, a form of execution much more violent and prolonged, was their goal. So they stirred up the crowd, using it to play on Pilate's fears and insecurities. It worked. They got what they wanted. Crucifixion, the Roman punishment, ended the life of a man who had never spoken a word against Rome or broken any of her laws.

Throughout the ordeal, Jesus was continuously denied his rights. As Frank Lake puts it:

> So little were the rights of Christ respected that He had to see His clothes raffled away by the soldiers throwing dice under the Cross. No magi here to bring costly gifts. No fish from the sea with the coin in its mouth to pay His taxes. No recognition of His right to any property at all, not even to His own coat and vest. This is how we treated the first-born of God's creation, by whom He made the worlds.[8]

In a world filled with inequities, with multitudes crying out "This is unfair. Where is the justice I deserve? Where are my rights?" we can assuredly say, "Jesus understands. He knows the rejection of unfair treatment."

The rejection of mockery. In *The Jesus I Never Knew,* Philip Yancey tells of Pierre Van Paassen's pre-World War II memoir describing an act of mockery and humiliation performed by Nazi storm troopers on an elderly Jewish rabbi who had been brought to their headquarters. There in the same room, while another Jew was being beaten to death, the rabbi was stripped naked and forced to preach the sermon he had prepared for the upcoming Sabbath. The rabbi meekly requested, in accordance with his tradition, to wear a yarmulke to cover his head. The Nazis readily agreed since it only added to the joke. He then proceeded to deliver his sermon on walking humbly before God, all the while being poked, prodded and ridiculed by the Nazis and compelled to listen to the desperate cries of his dying neighbor.

Yancey says that whenever he reads the Gospel accounts of Jesus' imprisonment, torture and death, "I think of that naked rabbi standing humiliated in a police station." But "I still cannot fathom the indignity [Christ] endured."[9]

The Gospel of Mark gives a graphic description of the mockery of Jesus at the cross:

> People passing along the road jeered, shaking their heads in mock lament: "You bragged that you could tear down the Temple and then rebuild it in three days—so show us your stuff! Save yourself! If you're really God's Son, come down from that cross!"
>
> The high priests, along with the religion scholars, were right there mixing it up with the rest of them, having a great time poking fun at him: "He saved others—but can't save himself! Messiah, is he? King of Israel? Then let him climb down from that cross. We'll *all* become believers then!" Even the men crucified alongside him joined in the mockery. (Mark 15:29-32 The Message)

Christ suffered taunts like this from the moment he appeared before the high priest until the darkness finally descended. He knew the rejection of mockery.

The rejection of physical abuse. In the final hours of his life, Christ experienced unimaginable physical abuse. He was flogged, spat on, struck in the face, garlanded with thorns, pierced by nails in his hands and feet, forced to support the full weight of his body for six hours, exposed and, finally, stabbed in his side with a spear to ensure he was dead.

In 1986, a few days prior to Holy Week, the *Journal of the American Medical Association* published an article titled "On the Physical Death of Jesus Christ," written by two physicians from the Mayo Clinic and a United Methodist pastor.[10] Assuming the accuracy of the Gospel accounts, the article examined Jesus' death from a medical point of view. The authors concluded that Jesus' death "resulted primarily from hypovolemic shock and exhaustion asphyxia." They included in their discussion a detailed description of the flogging of Jesus (Matthew 27:26; Mark 15:15; John 19:1).

Flogging was a legal preliminary to most Roman executions, and Jesus was no exception. The short whip used on victims consisted of several leather thongs to which small iron balls, sheep bones or metal spikes were fixed. The victims were stripped of their clothing, and their hands were tied to an upright post. The article describes the excruciating procedure:

> As the Roman soldiers repeatedly struck the victim's back with full force, the iron balls would cause deep contusions, and the leather thongs and sheep bones would cut into the skin and subcutaneous tissues. Then, as the flogging continued, the lacerations would tear into the underlying skeletal muscles and produce quivering ribbons of bleeding flesh. Pain and blood loss generally set the stage for circulatory shock. The extent of blood loss may well have determined how long the victim would survive on the cross.[11]

The blows Jesus endured enable him to identify with all who have suffered extreme physical abuse. He was despised and rejected—and neglected, deserted, betrayed, treated unfairly, mocked and physically abused. But the worst was yet to come: he would suffer abandonment and rejection even by God. He endured the full breadth of every form of rejection experienced by humans to a depth we cannot fathom.

BEARING OUR REJECTION AND DEFINING OUR WORTH

Because he experienced rejection firsthand in so many and such profound ways, Jesus can fully identify with us in our rejection. "Touched with the feeling of our infirmities" (Hebrews 4:15 KJV), he is therefore able to sympathize with us.

So bring your rejection to the cross. Reconsider what has happened to you in the light of what happened to him. Gaze at your wounds, then gaze at his, our fellow sufferer who understands.

But again I must emphasize, Jesus not only identifies with us in our rejection, he also participates in it. On the cross our rejection was mysteriously laid upon him. In his body on the tree he has borne both our sins (1 Peter 2:24) and our griefs and sorrows (Isaiah 53:4 NKJV), including our rejections.

You may have carried the grief and sorrow of rejection for years. Now as you stand before the cross, hear Jesus saying, "Give it all to me. Let me bear your rejection in my broken body. Let me absorb the pain into myself. Give me the hurtful words, the lonely times you were neglected, the occasions you felt let down or betrayed. Give me the abuse. Let me bear the brunt of your rejections. Let my wounds of rejection touch and carry yours."

The cross also addresses the results of rejection. Because others reject us, we find it difficult to accept ourselves. They consider us unlovable, so we consider ourselves unlovable too. At the cross, however, God's opinion of us stands fully revealed. We are of inestimable value to God. Accepted in Jesus the Beloved, we are loved beyond all measure, even worth dying for. As Paul declares, "God proves his love for us in that while we still were sinners Christ died for us" (Romans 5:8).

The cross proclaims that when you and I were at our worst, God loved us the most. We may have been rejected by others and tempted to despise ourselves, but we are infinitely loved by God. The cross settles the issue once and for all. No matter how others may define us or how we may be tempted to define ourselves, God has pronounced the final verdict: Accepted through his blood.

My friend Dick McClain, an executive with the Mission Society for United Methodists, tells about ministering to Jackie, a single mother who worked as a waitress in a local diner. She had come to know Christ through the witness of two men who met there regularly for breakfast and prayer. Following her conversion, she joined the church Dick pastored and began to seek counsel with him.

When she was a young girl, Jackie's father had sexually abused her. The wounds of those childhood experiences had produced a deep sense of self-loathing in her and led to an adulthood of promiscuity. However, as she grew in her new-found faith in Christ and counseled with her pastor, God enabled her not only to forgive her father but also to forgive herself. As a result, God was mending her brokenness, and she was beginning to love and accept herself.

Then one day Jackie literally burst into Dick's office. She sobbed and shook as she recounted what had happened the day before. Her father had been waiting for her when she arrived home. He had deliberately come at a time when he knew they would be alone. Then he had proceeded to force himself on her, threatening to molest Jackie's twelve-year-old daughter if she didn't submit to him. Terrified for her daughter and trapped once again by her childhood nightmare, Jackie froze as her own father once again assaulted her.

The horror of that violent experience threw Jackie back into an abyss of despair, shattering her growing self-esteem. Waves of worthlessness swept over her. All the progress she had made was seemingly reversed.

As Dick listened to Jackie he was silently praying. What could he possibly say that wouldn't seem trite in such a tragic situation? But the Holy Spirit prompted him to do something unusual. Inviting

Jackie to accompany him, he led her out of his office and into the sanctuary. They walked together down the center aisle until they stood facing the cross that hung over the chancel.

"Jackie," Dick said emphatically, "I want you to look at the cross. All your life you've believed a lie about who you are and what you are worth. Your father's despicable actions when you were a child and then yesterday are a part of the lie. Satan, the father of lies, has used those things to convince you that you're worthless and no good.

"Jackie, look at the cross. It's the only place in all the universe where you'll find the truth about yourself. Jesus died for you. That's how much he thinks you are worth. He loves you so much he gave his life for you. Look at the cross, Jackie, look at the cross."

As she gazed at the cross, the truth revealed there penetrated Jackie's heart and mind. She rejected the lie of her own worthlessness and believed the truth that she was in fact loved and worthwhile. The cloud of despair and self-loathing began to dissipate.

Jackie walked out of the sanctuary that day a changed person. Derailed by what had happened, she saw herself in the light of the cross and, bathed in that redeeming light, got back on track. In the months following, she continued to progress in her healing and faith journey.

Accepted. Beloved. Of infinite worth to God. That's what the cross tells us about ourselves. No rejection, anywhere or anytime, can ever change that.

QUESTIONS FOR PERSONAL OR GROUP REFLECTION

1. In what ways have you felt the sting of rejection? Has it been blatant and direct as in the case of abuse, or has it taken a more subtle, indirect form such as parental neglect?

2. Which of your experiences of rejection have wounded you most deeply? How have they affected your view of yourself? your relationships with others?

3. Jesus experienced rejection to its full depth and breadth. In particular, he suffered the pains of neglect, disloyalty, betrayal, unfairness, mockery and physical abuse. Through which of these forms of rejection do you sense the Lord Jesus identifying with you? What difference does it make in your memories of rejection to know that Jesus has truly been with you in that suffering?

4. When Jackie experienced recurring abuse from her earthly father, she believed the father of lies who told her that she was worthless. As she looked at the cross where Jesus died for her, she recognized the worth that Jesus placed on her life and came to believe that she was loved and worthwhile. Have you ever found yourself at a similar crossroad of belief? What lie have you been told through your experiences of rejection, and what does the cross have to say about it?

Disregarding the Shame

Shame is overcome only in the enduring of an act of final shaming. . . . Shame is overcome only in the shaming through the forgiveness of sin, that is to say, through the restoration of fellowship with God and men.

DIETRICH BONHOEFFER

Fyodor Dostoyevsky's magical novel *The Idiot* contains a wild and tragic character named Nastasia Philapovna. Nastasia delights in seducing men both young and old with her charm and captivating beauty. After an hour in her presence, they fall madly in love with her. But Nastasia delights even more in leaving them ungratified. She sleeps with them during the night but before dawn sneaks away laughing, leaving them pining for more of her love. Naturally, she is despised by other women, who are both jealous and afraid of her.

Only Prince Mishkin, the hero and Christ-figure in the story, can see deeply enough into her soul to understand what motivates her strange behavior. Nastasia is driven by a ferocious, self-destructive sense of shame.

As an abandoned, homeless child, Nastasia was taken in by a wealthy patron. He abused her and then kept her around like an ornament on a shelf that he could take down and occasionally fondle. The shame of being abandoned, abused and misused in this way had seared her soul. Mishkin explains how Nastasia's wildness was fueled by shame:

> Oh, don't cry shame upon her, don't throw stones at her! She has tortured herself too much from the consciousness of her undeserved shame. . . . She had an irresistible inner craving to do something shameful, so as to say to herself at once, "There, you've done something shameful again, so you're a degraded creature." . . . Do you know that in that continual conscious- ness of shame there is perhaps a sort of awful unnatural enjoy- ment for her, a sort of revenge on someone?[1]

Although *The Idiot* was written more than a century and a half ago, long before psychologists came to understand the far-reaching effects of shame, Dostoyevsky's insights are profoundly accurate. Shame, growing out of deep-seated human hurts, can wreak havoc in our lives and lies at the root of much self-destructive behavior. Like infection in a wound, it festers long after the injury occurs. Sometimes, as in the case of Nastasia, it can take on a life of its own.

But shame isn't always negative.

POSITIVE AND NEGATIVE SHAME

Shame can be both positive and negative. Our capacity for shame is God-given and reflects the glory bestowed on us by our Creator. Only noble beings, who can discriminate between good and evil and show respect for God, others and themselves, can feel shame. John Bradshaw underscores the importance of proper shame:

> It is necessary to have the feeling of shame if one is to be truly human. . . . Shame tells us our limits. Shame keeps us in our human boundaries, letting us know that we can and will make mistakes, and that we need help. Our shame tells us that we are not God. Healthy shame is the psychological foundation of hu- mility. It is the source of spirituality.[2]

In the Garden, Adam and Eve walked around naked yet un-ashamed (Genesis 2:25). They felt no shame because their relation-ship with God and one another was one of perfect trust. Later, when, in seeking to be like God (Genesis 3:5), they disobeyed and ate of the forbidden fruit, the *first* consequence of their action was to feel shame. "Then the eyes of both were opened, and they knew that they were naked; and they sewed fig leaves together and made loin-cloths for themselves" (Genesis 3:7).

When Adam and Eve broke trust with God, shame flooded over them. Like a flashing warning light, shame alerted them to the fact that something was wrong. At that point, they could have heeded the warning, faced up to what they had done, and turned to God in brokenness and repentance. Their broken trust would have begun to mend, and their shame would have helped restore relationship.

But how did they respond to shame? They began by hesitating. Plagued by terrifying self-doubt, they no longer felt confident to stand before God and each other unadorned and naked. Hesitating, in turn, led to hiding: "I was afraid, because I was naked; and I hid myself" (Genesis 3:10). They hid from God, each other, even from themselves. Then, to maintain their hiding places, they engaged in hurling. "She gave me fruit from the tree. . . . The serpent tricked me" (Genesis 3:12-13). Unsure of their own worth, they were afraid to acknowledge the truth about themselves. So they directed attention away from themselves by pointing fingers at someone else (Adam blamed Eve; Eve blamed the serpent). As a result, the breach in their relationship with God and with each other widened. Shame reaped a deadly harvest.

This destructive kind of shame, especially the shame rooted in our painful hurts and our sinful, unhealthy reactions to those hurts, distorts and destroys our God-given glory, rather than re-flecting it.

DYNAMICS OF DESTRUCTIVE SHAME

Lewis Smedes describes shame as "a very heavy feeling." Its heaviness is rooted in the awareness "that we do not measure up and maybe never will measure up to the sorts of persons we are meant to be." Thus shame "gives us a vague disgust with ourselves, which in turn feels like a hunk of lead on our hearts."[3]

Notice that Smedes says we feel shame's heaviness "on our hearts," at the very core of our being. In the Bible, a person's face represents his or her personal identity; it sets that person apart from others. No wonder then that shame is often described in terms of how it affects a person's face or countenance. For example, Isaiah declares:

No longer shall Jacob be ashamed,
    no longer shall his face grow pale. (Isaiah 29:22)

Shame is bound up with who we are, not merely with what we do. This is what distinguishes it from guilt. Guilt is about our behavior. Shame, though it may be triggered by something we have said or done, is about our being. I may have paid the fine and thus cancelled the guilt incurred by my traffic violation, but I may continue to feel shame for being the flawed person who did such a stupid thing.

This is why shame is so destructive. As psychologist Robert Karen puts it:

It is crippling, because it contains not just the derisive accusation that one is a wimp, a bully, a runt, or a fag but the further implication that one is at core a deformed being, fundamentally unlovable and unworthy of membership in the human community.

It is the self regarding the self with the withering and unforgiving eye of contempt. And most people are unable to face it. It is too annihilating.[4]

The shame of nakedness. At the core of shame is an acute feeling of self-exposure. Adam and Eve's eyes were opened and they knew that they were naked (Genesis 3:7). Shame painfully exposes our nakedness. Who we are—our ugliness, our foolishness, our deficiencies—stands revealed for all to see. The exposure is disorienting; we feel powerless, out of control. Like Adam and Eve, we rush to find fig leaves for covering and trees to hide behind. Shame is so distressing we will go to great lengths to avoid it.

But for those who have experienced deep-seated rejection, the heaviness of shame cannot be evaded. It is a pervasive, permanent cloud that always hangs over them. Karen describes such "pathological shame" as "an irrational sense of defectiveness, a feeling not of having crossed to the wrong side of the boundary but of having been born there."[5] John Bradshaw's description of "toxic shame" is similar:

> Toxic shame, the shame that binds you, is experienced as the all-pervasive sense that I am flawed and defective as a human being. Toxic shame is no longer an emotion that signals our limits, it is a state of being, a core identity. Toxic shame gives you a sense of worthlessness, a sense of failing and falling short as a human being. Toxic shame is a rupture of the self with the self.[6]

He maintains that such virulent shame fuels all addictive behaviors. Because the painful self-exposure is too much to bear, people turn to drugs, work, food, sex or some other safe, self-created world of numbness in order to find relief and acceptance.

The shame of worshiping false gods. But shame not only exposes the nakedness of our fragile selves, understood biblically, it also exposes the impotence of the false gods we worship and trust. When Adam and Eve accepted the serpent's lie, they bowed down to the false gods of wisdom ("knowing good and evil"), immortality ("you will not die") and pride ("you will be like God"). Thus they worshiped created things rather than the Creator (Romans 1:25).

When they ate the fruit their eyes *were* opened, just as the serpent had said. But instead of becoming like God, as the snake promised, they only discovered how naked, how un-Godlike they were.

Shame always exposes our misplaced trust in false gods, gods that are impotent and incapable of fulfilling their false promises. Isaiah proclaims:

> They shall be turned back and utterly put to shame—
>> those who trust in carved images,
> who say to cast images,
>> "You are our gods." (42:17)

Dan Allender tells of counseling Sean, a young man who had been sexually abused by his older brother. Every time Sean spoke or even thought about the abuse, shame's fires burned within him. But what about the abuse ignited the flames?

As they talked together, Sean's hatred of weakness and desire emerged. In response to being disappointed and let down by others when he was a young boy, Sean had constructed a thick protective wall around his heart. He vowed he would never need anything from anyone *except* his older brother.

Sean's older brother was everything he wanted to be: handsome, athletic and intelligent. Sean longed to be noticed by him and spend time with him. One night, after they had spent several hours together, his brother offered to teach him how to masturbate. While he was doing that, he asked Sean to stimulate him. Wanting to please him, Sean complied with his brother's request.

Afterward, Sean despised himself for what he had done and hated his brother for putting him in such an awkward position. Shame blanketed him. But as Allender explains:

> The origin of the shame that Sean felt was the exposure of the desperate trust he invested in his brother to provide what no person or thing can do—rescue and redeem. Rather than face

the foolishness of trusting his brother as a god, Sean hated himself for his weakness and desire. He had exchanged his old idol—his brother—for a new and even more pernicious god: freedom from weakness and desire.

Whenever he recalled the past abuse or experienced desire that seemed odd or excessive, he retreated into shame and then into vicious self-hatred.[7]

Some of the shame we feel comes as a result of the victimizing sins of others. What they have done can cause us to believe we are inherently flawed. But we also feel shame because of our own sins and idolatries. We bow down to false gods such as control, safety, approval, power, freedom, perfectionism and invincibility, and we are "put to shame" when they fail to deliver.

THE SHAME OF THE CROSS

The author of Hebrews exhorts us to fix our eyes on Jesus, "the pioneer and perfecter of our faith." For the joy that was set before him he "endured the cross, disregarding its shame" (Hebrews 12:2). We already looked at certain aspects of the excruciating physical pain Jesus endured when he was crucified (for example, flogging). But people in Roman times dreaded the shame of crucifixion even more than the physical pain of it.

Crucifixion was reserved for those on the bottom rung of the social ladder such as slaves, hardened criminals and enemies of the state. Roman citizens condemned to death were usually beheaded; their executions were over and done with quickly. They were *never* crucified; it was considered too horrible and degrading.

To determine the significance of crucifixion in the ancient world, New Testament scholar Martin Hengel meticulously searched for references to it in classical literature and inscriptions but found relatively few. Although the practice was widespread, especially in Roman times, "the cultured literary world wanted to have nothing to do with it, and as a rule kept quiet about it"[8] *Cross* was a vulgar word not used in polite company. According to Cicero, the great Roman statesman and philosopher, the word was so vulgar that Roman citizens should never even mention it: "It should never pass through their thoughts, eyes, or ears."[9]

Crucifixions were purposely carried out in public, generally at some prominent place like a crossroads, an outdoor theater or a hill. Ancient authors often describe them as spectacle events. Executioners heightened the shame and disgrace by turning the gruesome personal ordeal into grisly public entertainment. The public mockery and ridicule heaped on Jesus during his crucifixion (Mark 15:29-32) was typical of most crucifixions.

In most paintings, films and artistic depictions, the crucified figure of Jesus is partially covered with a loincloth. But in the ancient world, the victim was always crucified naked. The shameful exposure often continued even after death since it was common for the victim to be denied burial. Hengel explains the shame associated with that denial in ancient times:

> It was a stereotyped picture that the crucified victim served as food for wild beasts and birds of prey. In this way his humiliation was made complete. What it meant for a man in antiquity to be refused burial, and the dishonor which went with it, can hardly be appreciated by modern man.[10]

Occasionally persons already dead were nailed to a cross. Unable to suffer physical pain, they were still subject to the degrading humiliation associated with crucifixion. No wonder the formula for sentencing people to crucifixion read, "Executioner, bind his hands, veil his head, and hang him on the tree of shame."[11] In heaping insult and disgrace on someone, nothing could compare to "the tree of shame."

Because of the horrendous shame associated with crucifixion, early hearers of the message of the cross (1 Corinthians 1:18) found it offensive. According to Paul, it was "a stumbling block to Jews and foolishness to Gentiles" (1 Corinthians 1:23). In Greek, the word translated "foolishness" is *moria*, from which we derive our English word "moron." For the typical Greek or Roman person, the Christian belief that someone who had been crucified was Savior and Lord of all was sheer madness. How could someone who had been hanged on the tree of shame be worthy of worship?

The Greek word for "stumbling block" is *skandalon*, from which we derive our English word "scandal." It was indeed scandalous to tell Jews that the long-awaited Messiah had been nailed to a cross, for they also believed crucifixion was a sign of God's curse. Torah was clear: "anyone hung on a tree is under God's curse" (Deuteronomy 21:23). How could a *cursed* one be the Messiah, God's *chosen* one? "Crucified messiah" was an oxymoron, a notion that was ludicrous and revolting.

OVERCOMING OUR SHAME

On the cross Jesus experienced such unfathomable shame and humiliation, such amazing disgrace, that it was extremely difficult for Jews and Gentiles to believe he was the Son of God. Yet those who have believed—in the first century and ever since—have found him to be "Christ the power of God and the wisdom of God" (1 Corinthians 1:24), the One who is sufficient for all things, even overcoming shame.

Because Christ willingly endured shame on the cross, we are able to find healing for our shame at the cross. Adam and Eve disobeyed God by eating fruit from an alluring tree in a garden. As a result, they were naked and ashamed. Jesus obeyed God while nailed to a shameful tree on a hill. As a result, we can stand before God, naked and unashamed. "A tree had destroyed us," said Theodore of Studios. "A tree now brought us life."

On the cross, Christ overcame the painful self-exposure bound up with shame by both identifying with and participating in our shame. Frank Lake expresses this truth powerfully in describing Christ's experience of the shame of nakedness:

> He hangs on the Cross naked. Both the innocent who were not loved and the guilty who have spurned love are ashamed. Both have something to hide. Clothing is the symbol of hiding what we are ashamed to reveal. In His own innocence He is identified with the innocent in nakedness. . . . He was so deprived of His natural clothing of transfigured beauty and glory that men, seeing Him thus, shrank away from Him. The whole world will see this same King appearing in all His beauty and glory, because He allowed both . . . to be utterly taken away.[12]

My father, David Seamands, tells of two sisters who attended a weekend seminar he was leading on emotional and spiritual wholeness.[13] Both had been sexually molested by an uncle and were extremely bitter toward him. At an afternoon session they became angry with Dad when he stressed the indispensable part forgiveness plays in healing. Was he suggesting they should forgive their uncle? How could he dare ask them to do that? How could God? Given what their uncle had done to them, didn't they have every right to be resentful? As far as they were concerned, forgiving him was out of the question. So was trusting God. As the older sister angrily exclaimed, "You're asking me to trust God? I tried that when I was six years old. I cried out to God to protect me from my uncle, but he didn't. The only thing I could do was cover my head with my pillow."

Wanting to respond sensitively, my dad thanked the sisters for their honest reaction. Then he felt prompted by the Spirit to describe several aspects of Christ's shameful abuse that paralleled theirs. During his trial, men blindfolded him (the King James Version says they "covered his face") and beat him with their fists (Mark 14:65). During his crucifixion, he experienced the shame and humiliation of nakedness.

In hearing this, the older sister felt deeply moved. She never realized Jesus had endured these things. It dawned on her that Jesus could identify with her and other victims of sexual abuse. Like her face covered with a pillow, his face had been covered. He too must have felt powerless and unprotected by God. She had been stripped of her clothing; so had he. He too had shameful indignities inflicted on his naked body.

Jesus could understand her hurt and anger. He knew why it was so hard for her to forgive her uncle. Jesus did not condemn her for her struggle. He wept for her and with her. He knew first-hand about the humiliation she had experienced. On the cross he bore the shame she experienced when her uncle molested her.

At the close of the next morning's session that sister came and knelt to receive prayer for healing. She told my father she was willing now to let go of her bitterness toward her uncle. She also wanted to begin trusting God again.

Knowing that Jesus knew her pain, understanding that he understood her shame broke through her resistance and softened her heart. As she prayed at the altar, bottled-up tears gushed forth, washing away layers of shame. Christ's wounds began to heal hers.

Unfortunately, her younger sister didn't respond in the same way but instead became even angrier. In fact, she felt betrayed that her sister left her to nurse her hurt and anger all by herself. For the younger sister, the cross was a stumbling block; for the older sister, it was the power of God (1 Corinthians 1:23-24). That same power is available for all who dare to believe. Through his identification and participation with us, he can overcome the self-exposure, the feeling of self-loathing bound up with shame.

The cross also addresses shame's exposure of our trust in false gods. For not only did Jesus bear shame on the cross, he also shamed shame. Shame itself was crucified on the cross. As Paul declares, "And having disarmed the powers and authorities, he made a public spectacle of them, triumphing over them by the cross" (Colossians 2:15 NIV).

By crucifying Jesus, the religious leaders and the Roman authorities sought to expose him. Remember how they ridiculed him as he hung there? "If you're a king, if you're the messiah, then come down from the cross. If you really are the Son of God, why doesn't God deliver you?" The fact that God didn't deliver him proved he was an imposter, not the messiah, as many were claiming.

But in spite of their taunting, Jesus kept trusting God. He disregarded the shame of the cross. Though he felt forsaken by God, he desperately held on to God. In the end he still believed God would vindicate him. And three days later God did. According to Paul, he was "declared to be Son of God" through his resurrection from the dead (Romans 1:4).

The powers and authorities made a public spectacle of him. But having endured the awful shame of the cross and having been vindicated by God, now the tables were turned. He made a public spectacle of them.

The religious leaders claimed they were God's representatives. The Roman authorities maintained God had appointed them to rule. Yet when confronted with God's own Son, did they acknowledge him? No. "For if they had, they would not have crucified the Lord of glory" (1 Corinthians 2:8). By crucifying him, their true nature was exposed, made public for all to see. They were *not* God's agents as they claimed, but God's adversaries, agents of false gods, of the principalities and powers.

Remember the story of the emperor's new clothes? When the brash little boy saw the emperor strut by in what were purported to be his royal robes, he cried out, "He's naked!" Jesus hung naked on the cross. And his nakedness exposed their nakedness. His great final act of being shamed overcame shame itself.

In the same way the cross exposed the false gods of the religious leaders and authorities and the emptiness of their misplaced trust, it exposes our false gods and misplaced trust. At the cross every false robe of pretence is stripped from us; our nakedness is revealed for all to see. Our wisdom is revealed as foolishness, our strength as weakness (1 Corinthians 1:25).

But, thank God, the cross also reveals about us what it revealed about Jesus. In spite of all the ridicule and shame heaped on him, in spite of the people's accusations and even his own feelings of God-forsakenness, he was not abandoned by God. Throughout his crucifixion his relationship with God remained intact. He was *still* the beloved Son in whom his Father was well-pleased (Matthew 3:17). And no matter how much shame we experience or how often we put our trust in false gods, we too are not abandoned. Our relationship as daughters and sons of God, his beloved children, is still intact. As Rodney Clapp puts it, "No shame, however just or unjust, however petty or spectacular, can 'separate us from the love of God in Christ Jesus our Lord' " (Romans 8:39)."[4]

Thus, instead of being bound by shame, we can abound with confident boldness. The New Testament speaks of the confidence—*parrhesia*—we have before Christ. This Greek word *parrhesia* is the opposite of shame. John says, "When He appears, we may have confidence [*parrhesia*] and not shrink away from Him in shame at His coming" (1 John 2:28 NASB). Other occurrences of *parrhesia* indicate that we not only possess confidence for the future, we also enjoy certainty in the present. We *are* confident because our heart does not condemn us (1 John 3:21), we are free from fear (1 John 4:17-18), our prayers are heard (1 John 5:14), and we can draw near to the throne of grace (Hebrews 4:16), even boldly enter the holy of holies by the blood of Jesus (Hebrews 10:19).

New Testament scholar Heinrich Schlier summarizes his study of the powerful New Testament word *parrhesia:* "He who is in Christ has found again freedom towards God and can approach God with confidence. He can stand before the Ruler and Judge free and erect, not lowering his head, able to bear His presence."[15]

Of course, the healing of the shame that binds us takes time. To expose, loosen and sever shame's tentacles often entails a long, drawn-out process. But thanks to Christ's death on the cross, shame can be overcome. Because Jesus bore it on Calvary, we no longer must bear it. Redeemed and restored by Christ, we need not shrink away or lower our head. We can now stand before God, as Adam and Eve did at creation's dawn, with confident boldness, naked and unashamed.

A GREAT BIG DROP OF BLOOD

Steve, a seminary student who had formerly been an evangelist in Australia, witnessed the dramatic power of the cross to overcome shame while he was leading a retreat for Christians in the Air, a Christian organization for airline personnel. During the final session of the retreat, he conducted an informal Communion service. The chairs in the room formed a large circle, and the Communion table stood in the center. As hymns and choruses were sung, those present came to the table to receive the bread and cup. A strong sense of God's presence filled the room.

As the service continued, Steve felt impressed to pray for a woman seated opposite him on the other side of the circle. Her refined, classic appearance and impeccable makeup and clothing made her stand out from the others. As he asked the Holy Spirit to guide him in praying for her, a Scripture verse came to his mind: "How much more will the blood of Christ, who through the eternal spirit offered himself without blemish to God, purify our conscience from dead works to worship the living God" (Hebrews 9:14).

Although Steve didn't know why, he began to intercede for the woman along the implications of that verse. "Lord," he prayed, "if there is shame and guilt in her life, if there's uncleanness—whatever she's struggling with, lift it off her. By your blood come and free this woman."

Suddenly, much to his surprise, the woman literally fell from her chair onto the floor and began sobbing uncontrollably. Some friends knelt beside her to comfort her. Not feeling prompted to join them, Steve simply sat where he was and kept praying for her.

Eventually the woman got up from the floor and sat back down. She seemed relieved but dazed. Soon afterward, the service ended. The retreat was over, and everyone quickly packed up and headed home. Since Steve's plane wasn't scheduled to leave until the next morning, he went to spend the night with the couple who had organized the retreat.

About ten o'clock that night, as Steve and the couple relaxed together in their home, they heard a knock at the door. It was the woman Steve had prayed for at the retreat. When he first saw her, Steve knew immediately that something was different about her appearance, but he couldn't determine what it was.

After she came in and sat down, she said to Steve, "I apologize for coming over here so late like this, but I just had to tell you what the Lord did for me during the Communion service.

"Before I committed myself to Christ a couple of years ago, I lived a very promiscuous life. As I sat there this afternoon, I began thinking about all the different men I'd slept with. My life was so messed up, that one night when I was drunk, I actually married someone. The next morning when I woke up, I didn't even know what I'd done. That's the kind of life I was living.

"And it was all rooted in my terrible shame. Because of what had happened when I was little, I felt utterly worthless and no good. I was ashamed to let anyone know who I really was—they would reject me if I did. Yet I needed their approval so desperately, especially the approval of men. I would do anything to get it.

"As a result, my whole life centered around my appearance. How people saw me, being attractive to men—those things meant everything to me and dominated my life. I couldn't even go to the corner store late at night to get a quart of milk without spending at least fifteen minutes in front of the mirror, making sure the makeup was just right and every hair was in place. I was a slave to that.

"After I came to know Christ a couple of years ago, I quit being promiscuous. But the guilt for the things I'd done and the shame about myself were still there. So was the overwhelming need for approval. I wasn't free from all that, but I desperately wanted to be. During the Communion service I pleaded with the Lord to come and do something for me."

Then she paused and looked sheepishly at Steve. "I don't know what you'll think of this, but while I was praying, I looked over at the corner of the room. There, suspended just below the ceiling, I saw this reddish cloud." She hesitated, "It looked like a great big drop of blood!

"I'm sure no one else saw it, but *I* did. As I stared at it, it slowly began to move toward me until it was hovering over me. And then it seemed to burst and came flooding down upon me! That's when I fell onto the floor sobbing. And I know it's strange, but I just had to tell you. While I was lying there Jesus came and washed me in his blood. He cleansed me. He freed me. And now my terrible sense of guilt and shame is gone!"

At that point, it finally dawned on Steve what was different about the woman. She didn't have on any makeup. Not that there's anything wrong with wearing makeup. But by not wearing it that night, she made a bold statement, witnessing to what Christ through his blood had done in her life. She no longer felt ashamed; she had nothing to hide. She could stand before God and others with confident boldness. Set free by his blood, her shame was gone.

Of course, she still faced a long journey toward wholeness. In place of her negative, shame-based thinking patterns, she had to develop new positive-thinking patterns based on her identity in Christ as a beloved daughter of God. Such change requires a gradual, deliberate process, but the turning point came in that crisis moment. Because of Christ's dramatic work in her life that day, she could begin the journey. Shame's binding shackles were broken. She was ready now—with confident boldness—to move toward becoming the woman God had destined her to be.

Is there shame in your life that needs to be brought to the cross of Christ? Do you see it, right now, wherever you are—a great big drop of blood?

QUESTIONS FOR PERSONAL OR GROUP REFLECTION

1. "Shame . . . lies at the root of much self-destructive behavior" (p. 42). Where have you observed this truth in yourself and in others?

2. Positive shame is like a warning light that shows us where we have done something wrong, leading us to turn to God with a contrite heart. Think of one or two examples of positive shame that led you to repentance and to restoration with God and others.

3. Negative shame is often rooted in the wrongs done to us and in our sinful, unhealthy reactions to them. Those burdened with negative shame are often driven to "drugs, work, food, sex or some other safe, self-created world of numbness" (p. 45) where they find temporary relief and a sense of the acceptance that they crave. Where has your negative shame driven you?

4. The author states that "shame always exposes our misplaced trust in false gods, gods that are impotent and incapable of fulfilling their false promises" (p. 46). Later he specifically mentions false gods of control, safety, approval, power, freedom, perfectionism

and invincibility (p. 47). Have you put your trust in any of these gods? How has shame revealed that these false gods do not deserve your trust?

5. What does it mean that Jesus was hung on a "tree of shame" and regarded as one who was "under God's curse"?

6. Have you ever had an experience of cleansing and release from shame similar to the woman who saw the big drop of blood? Do you long, as she did, to be released from shame and guilt? Do you need to humbly invite Jesus to meet you in some place of shame?

4

Why Have You Forsaken Me?

Anyone who thinks about disappointment with God must pause at Gethsemane, and at Pilate's palace, and at Calvary—the scenes of Jesus' arrest, trial, and execution. For in those three places Jesus himself experienced a state very much like disappointment with God.

PHILIP YANCEY

About fifteen ministers sat in a circle in the class I was teaching. We were discussing why we spend so little time in prayer when suddenly, one man began to sob. I was puzzled. Nothing had been said to prompt such an emotional response, so I wondered if he was struggling with a personal problem.

"Is there something you'd like us to pray with you about?" I asked.

"Oh no," he replied. "It's nothing like that. During this discussion God has been showing me why it's been so difficult for me to pray the last few years.

"About five years ago," he went on to explain, "I came home and found a note on the kitchen table from my wife. She said she didn't want to be my wife anymore. So she had taken her things and left.

"I was devastated—I didn't think this could ever happen to me. And what was going to happen to my ministry?

"In the months that followed I pleaded with God about our marriage. 'Lord, you can't let this separation end in a divorce. I know that's not your will. You've got to save my marriage.' I prayed like that constantly. And I was convinced—I just *knew* God was going to come through."

Then he shook his head. "God didn't save our marriage. It ended in divorce. And today I realized for the first time how my deep hurt, and especially my disappointment with God over my divorce, has affected my desire to pray. I felt so let down by God. I got burned so badly when God didn't come through. And when you've gotten burned once like that, you sure don't want to get burned twice.

"I have no problem praying for others," he continued. "I can encourage them to trust God. But when it comes to myself and my needs, it's so hard to pray. I'm afraid I'll get hurt again. I know I should pray—so I force myself. But then I'm flooded with doubts. Does God really listen to my prayers? Does God care about my needs? I can't say I'm sure anymore."

Both rejection and shame had stabbed this man's heart. His wife had walked out on him; his marriage had failed. He would forever bear the stigma of divorce. But what he said that day centered around another issue that often arises in relation to our hurts: disappointment with God. John Stott maintains that "the real sting of suffering is not misfortune itself, nor even the pain or the injustice of it, but the apparent God-forsakenness of it. Pain is endurable, but the seeming indifference of God is not."[1]

According to Scripture, God loves us "with an everlasting love" (Jeremiah 31:3); God is

> faithful in all his words,
>   and gracious in all his deeds. (Psalm 145:13)

We should therefore "trust in him at all times" (Psalm 62:8). Because the Lord is our shepherd, we have everything we need (Psalm 23). He provides green pastures and still waters for us; he protects so no evil or enemy can harm us. Yet does God *always* provide and protect the way the familiar Twenty-Third Psalm might lead us to expect? No. And that's when we feel the sting of disappointment with God.

Virginia knew the sting. And as a result, she dropped out of church. In fact, she hadn't attended worship in fifteen years. But a few months after I was appointed pastor at the church, she unexpectedly showed up one Sunday morning and kept coming back.

One afternoon I stopped by her home to visit. After we had talked awhile I said, "Everyone in the congregation is so glad you've returned. They've told me what an active member you once were. But I'm curious, why did you stop coming to church?"

"It's true," she replied. "I was very active. I taught Sunday school. My husband and I, our two young children—we were there whenever the doors were open. Then one day, right here in this room, my husband, who was only forty, had a massive heart attack. He keeled over in front of me and was dead before the ambulance could get him to the hospital.

"I was devastated," she went on. "At the time I wasn't working. My husband was the sole breadwinner. Now it was up to me to provide for the family. I felt so frightened and alone, so abandoned by God. One day in anger, I shook my fist at God and cried 'This isn't fair. I've been trying to follow you and serve you. How could you let this happen?'

"So I turned away from God and quit coming to church. That was fifteen years ago, and now I regret what I did. But it's taken me all these years to get past my hurt and anger. I'm finally ready to open my heart to God again."

Before I left her home, we prayed for the healing of her wounded heart and restoration of her relationship with God. But as I drove away I found myself thinking, *How tragic! All those years of fellowship with Christ and his church—lost because of what happened. What long-term consequences can result from disappointments with God.*

THE EFFECTS OF DISAPPOINTMENT WITH GOD

What effects do such experiences have on our relationship with God? Let's consider three of the most common.

1. *Disappointments with God damage our trust receptors.* The minister who felt let down because God didn't save his marriage said it well: "When you've been burned once, you sure don't want to get burned twice. . . . I'm afraid of getting hurt again."

Imagine you are alone in a small chapel, praying about a problem you've been wrestling with. As you are praying, God speaks to you: "Turn your problem over to me. Trust me to work it out. And as an expression of your faith, get up from your pew, go to the Communion table, and grasp hold of the metal crucifix on it. Lift it up off the table. Hold it tightly." So as an act of trust and obedience, you walk forward to the table and take hold of the cross.

Now imagine someone else—for example, a woman in her thirties—praying in that same chapel about some issue in her life. She hears God saying the same thing to her: "As an expression of your trust in me, go to the Communion table and take hold of the cross." But unlike you, imagine the woman has a deep cut in the palm of her hand. Even slightly bending her fingers causes her to grimace with pain. If she takes hold of the cross, it will be almost unbearable. The cut in her hand makes her act of faith extremely difficult.

Those who have encountered disappointment with God often have deep cuts in their hands. Damaged trust receptors make it painful to reach out to God. Memories of past disappointments convince them God will *always* be indifferent. They also stir up shame. Feeling that God abandoned them confirms they are worthless.

2. *Disappointments with God fuel anger at God.* Like the woman whose husband died of a sudden heart attack, we want to cry out against God when we feel abandoned, "How could you allow that? It was so unfair. Why didn't you stop it from happening? Why weren't you there to help us?"

Years after some painful experience, we may still be angrily clenching our fist at God without even realizing it. During a Saturday evening service, the pastor of a church where I was leading a spiritual renewal weekend shared with his congregation how the Lord had been speaking to him. He was in his mid-thirties, but that morning in a workshop, as I was discussing anger with God, he saw himself as a heartbroken, thirteen-year-old boy. His parents were getting a divorce. Tears streamed down his cheeks as he stood on the front porch and watched his father drive away from home for the last time.

"All these years I've been angry at God for that," he confessed. "I was mad at God for not keeping my parents together, and I was not even aware of it. Now I see how it's been affecting my ability to trust and receive God's love."

As a result of anger fueled by disappointments, many sincere Christians work at cross purposes with themselves. One hand is open, reaching upward toward God. The words of an ancient prayer express the deep longing they have for a closer relationship with God: "To see Thee more clearly, love Thee more dearly, and follow Thee more nearly." But the other hand is a clenched fist raised upward against God. It's as if they are driving a car with one foot on the accelerator while the other is on the brake! Their unresolved anger undercuts their desire for spiritual growth.

3. *Disappointments with God expose our idols.* We saw earlier how shame is often bound up with the false gods we worship. The same holds true of our disappointments.

On the wall in my home office hangs a framed Scripture verse: "Delight yourself in the Lord and he will give you the desires of your heart" (Psalm 37:4 NIV). This wonderful verse encourages us to make the Lord our focus and our joy. If we do, God promises to fulfill our heart's desires. But often we reverse the order and live by our own version: "Delight yourself in the desires of your heart—and ask the Lord to give them to you." In other words, we serve God in order to get what we want. We assume that in exchange for our service God is obligated to grant our desires.

What happens when God doesn't fulfill them? We feel let down, sometimes even betrayed. We were counting on God, but God didn't come through. Yet the truth is, no matter what we assumed when we signed on as disciples, God never promised to pander to our selfish desires.

So our disappointments with God are often the children of our false expectations. And behind our false expectations lurk the idols, the false gods we worship.

After graduation, a seminarian returned to pastor a church in his home state and denomination. He already knew and loved many of the pastors there and was thrilled to be considered their colleague. He assumed that a promising ministerial career lay ahead of him.

But what he thought would be a great start to his career turned into a jolting, dream-shattering experience. Through a very unusual set of circumstances, he fell victim to harsh and unfair treatment by his colleagues and those in authority over him. Consequently, he was forced out of both his church and the denomination. Broken and disillusioned, he moved to another state.

The healing of his deep wounds took place slowly, dragging out over the next four years. Coming to terms with his disappointment with God played a significant part in his healing. Gradually, his deep-seated anger at God was diffused, and his shattered trust was restored.

One day as he was praying, he realized how much he had lived for the acceptance and approval of his ministerial colleagues. His status and reputation in the denomination had meant everything to him. He had fashioned an idol out of it. Now at last he realized why he was so disappointed and angry with God: instead of supporting his idol, God had allowed it to be smashed.

Tears of repentance welled up in his eyes. "Oh, God," he cried, "forgive me for wanting their affirmation and favor even more than yours." Soon his tears of grief were mixed with tears of gratitude. "Thank you, Lord," he prayed. "You loved me so much, you wouldn't allow me to live with the illusion I could find ultimate satisfaction in anything other than you." By allowing his idol to be destroyed, God had refined his motives and purified his love.

BRINGING OUR DISAPPOINTMENT WITH GOD TO THE CROSS

As he hung on the cross, Jesus himself felt disappointed, even abandoned by God. After being suspended for six hours, he finally voiced his disappointment. According to Mark's account, he cried out "with a loud voice, 'Eloi, Eloi, lema sabachthani?' "(15:34). In Aramaic—the language he actually spoke—Jesus was reciting a familiar verse, Psalm 22:1: "My God, My God, why have you forsaken me." In his bitter cry of dereliction, he made those words his own.

But not only did Jesus cry out for himself, he cried out for us too. He gave expression to all of humanity's—all of creation's (Romans 8:22)—groaning cries of disappointment with God. On the cross, our cries are both anticipated and caught up in his.

Of course, Jesus wasn't the first righteous person to voice disappointment with God. The Bible offers numerous examples, especially in Psalms and the book of Job. Still, many Christians hesitate to express their disappointment. "If God has allowed something to happen, what right do you have to cry out against it?" they have been told. Better then to resign ourselves to what God has ordained, to accept it, no questions asked. Churches are not often places where people feel free to voice disappointment with God or raise hard questions. Those who dare to do so are frequently shamed into silence.

But if Jesus openly and loudly cried, "My God, my God, why?" shouldn't that give us permission to cry out? Pierre Wolff says, "If Jesus in all his perfection had the audacity to ask his Father, 'Why?'

we can express to God all our whys, since the why of the Son of Man embraced ours. None of our whys can be excluded from his, because all of our whys are healed through his."[2]

Wolff goes on to make an intriguing suggestion: Jesus cried out not only as the Son of Man but also as the Son of God. His why was also God's why over the sin and suffering of creation. Furthermore, since we who are in Christ are also sons and daughters of God, there may be times, through the groaning of the Spirit in us (Romans 8:26-28), when our whys are actually God's too. In such cases "our revolt expresses the Father's own revolt rather than human rebellion against him. We think we are accusing him, while in reality he is sorrowfully questioning the world through us!"[3]

Wolff writes of a time he witnessed this when he was comforting a couple whose son had been killed in a senseless accident. The boy's mother was openly voicing her disappointment and anger against God over their son's death. The father, on the other hand, believed they should trust God by humbly and silently resigning themselves to it.

At first Wolff was uncomfortable with the mother's protests. The father's faith seemed much stronger than hers. But as they continued to talk, his perception of her negative feelings changed. "All of a sudden I understood that she was to us a witness to the sorrow of God." So he said to her, "Do not accuse the Lord; he is probably thinking the same thing you are. Do not think you are against him; he is beside you, speaking through you. Our Father has also 'lost' a child."[4] When she heard those words, a deep peace engulfed the woman.

"My God, my God, why have you forsaken me?" On the cross, Christ gave expression not only to his own sorrow and disappointment, and ours, but also to God's. His cry of dereliction is therefore an invitation to boldly voice our disappointments with God. At the foot of the cross our mournful cries of lament are welcome.

OVERCOMING THE EFFECTS OF
DISAPPOINTMENT WITH GOD

I said earlier that disappointments with God can damage our trust receptors, fuel our anger and expose our idols. Interestingly, all three of these issues are present in the drama of Christ's crucifixion. At Calvary, Jesus' faith is tested as never before (trust). He is the object of the people's rage (anger), which is fueled by their self-serving expectations of a political messiah (idolatry). Let's examine these one at a time.

Damaged trust. On the cross Jesus struggled to maintain his trust in God. As he hung there, the religious leaders taunted, "He trusts in God; let God deliver him now, if he wants to; for he said, 'I am God's Son' " (Matthew 27:43). But God *didn't* deliver him. God seemed indifferent. That Friday there was darkness at noon, thick darkness that hid the sun and also hid God's face. No voice from heaven this time—only silence, until Jesus cried out, "My God, my God, why . . . ?"

This cry is the only place in the Gospels where Jesus doesn't address God with the personal, intimate "My Father," but instead uses the more formal, distant "My God." What he had struggled with in Gethsemane, what he had implored his Father to save him from, had at last come upon him. In Golgatha's deep darkness, he felt forsaken by the One he had always called Father, the One who had called him his Beloved Son. Centuries earlier, the prophet Amos poignantly described the scene:

> On that day, says the Lord God,
> > I will make the sun go down at noon,
> > and darken the earth in broad daylight. . . .
> I will make it like the mourning for an only son,
> > and the end of it like a bitter day. (Amos 8:9-10)

On the cross, the bonds of trust between the Father and the Son seem to disintegrate. As theologian Jürgen Moltmann says, "The love that binds the one to the other is transformed into a dividing curse."[5] In that awful experience, as the Son bears the sins of the world, and the Father, whose eyes are too pure to look on evil (Habakkuk 1:13), turns his face away, God seems mysteriously divided from God. God forsakes God. In Martin Luther's words, we see "God striving with God." Separated from each other, the relationship between the Father and the Son seems to break off.

Yet at the cross, the Father and the Son are never more united, never more bound together. They are one in their surrender, one in their self-giving. The Father surrenders the Son. As Paul says, God "did not withhold his own Son, but gave him up for all of us" (Romans 8:32). The Son, in turn, surrenders himself to the will of the Father. He

became obedient to the point of death—
even death on a cross. (Philippians 2:8)

So the Father and the Son are united even in their separation, held together by their oneness of will and purpose.

"Father, into your hands I commend my spirit" (Luke 23:46). In his final utterance from the cross, Jesus reaffirms his connection to God. These words, also from the Psalms (31:5), were commonly recited by Jewish children as a now-I-lay-me-down-to-sleep bedtime prayer. Jesus probably learned them at Mary's knee. His last words, then, are an affirmation of faith. He addresses God as Father once again, thus implying he is the Son. He places himself in God's hands. As the Scripture says, "He entrusted himself to the one who judges justly" (1 Peter 2:23).

So the religious leaders were right in saying, "He trusts in God." He did. When he felt utterly God-forsaken, his faith may have faltered, but it did not fail. He died with a prayer of childlike faith on his lips.

As we bring our damaged trust receptors to the cross, consider what his faith can mean for us. In Galatians 2:19-20, Paul declares that we "have been crucified with Christ." Consequently, we no longer live, but Christ now lives in us; and the life we now live, we live "by faith in the Son of God." That last phrase can also be translated "by the faith *of* the Son of God."

Of course, there is truth in both translations, but in the light of damaged trust receptors that make our faith *in* the Son of God difficult, the faith *of* the Son of God takes on special significance. At the foot of the cross, his faith—which endured to the end—can be imparted to us. A wonderful exchange takes place: our damaged trust for his determined faith. The exchange may happen suddenly, but usually it comes gradually. We may stand beneath the cross with our damaged trust receptors for a long time. No matter how long it takes, we can rest assured: the faith *of* the Son of God will be passed on to us, enabling us to trust again. In a phrase from one of Fanny Crosby's hymns, "Cords that are broken will vibrate once more."[6]

Anger against God. Suspended on the cross, Jesus was the focus of anger on the part of the religious leaders, the soldiers and the common people. Even one of the thieves being crucified with him turned against him. From Jesus' arrest through his crucifixion, their hostility toward him poured out as they mocked him, spit in his face, flogged him, shook their fists at him and drove in the nails. At the cross it was not "sinners in the hands of an angry God" but "God in the hands of angry sinners." Christ became the willing, innocent victim of their rage.

But not only their rage—ours too. Frank Lake is right: "We attended the Crucifixion in our crowds, turned on the Healer, strengthening the hands of His persecutors, yelling, full of *rage* and spite, 'Crucify Him.' Our rage is focused on Him as they hammer the nails through the bones and use them to peg Him up."[7]

"Were you there when they crucified my Lord?" Yes, we *were* there—the entire human race—all of us. Martin Luther said we carry his nails in our pockets. Our anger at God's failure to deliver us and our indignant protests over life's injustices emerged in full force at the foot of the cross. There we stood, enraged murderers of God and yet—what wondrous love is this—as the beloved of God too.

What then should we do with our anger fueled by disappointment with God? Christians often hesitate to admit they are angry at God, and they are even more hesitant to openly express that anger. However, the cross boldly proclaims that no matter how intense or explosive our anger, it cannot separate us from God's love. The cross proves there is nothing you can't express to God. You can shake your fist, spit, rant and rave, spew out your bitterness, vent your rage at God—it really doesn't matter. Because it's already been done—on Good Friday. And since *you* were there, you've already done it—yet God still loves you!

The cross proclaims that our anger does not intimidate God. He is able to handle it. In fact, the cross is the great anger absorber of the universe. The rage, the anger of all humanity against God, was borne in Christ's broken body. The cross, then, is a safe place to bring our anger against God. There we can own it; we can admit that we're angry at God. And then we can disown it and give it to Christ there. Instead of carrying the anger ourselves or venting it on others, we can let him carry it for us.

At one of the healing services being held on the seminary campus where I work, a woman named Carol came forward to receive prayer. I had counseled with her several times prior to that service, and I knew she was beginning to realize how angry she was at God because of past hurts and injustices. "How can I pray for you?" I asked her when she came forward. She shook her index finger in my face and muttered fiercely, "I hate God—I hate *your* God."

There was a time when her answer would have unsettled me. But knowing what I knew about her and about the cross, I found her straightforward response refreshing and full of promise. "Let's bring that to the cross now," I suggested. "Your confession that you hate God—let that be your offering, your sacrifice of praise tonight."

What I suggested puzzled her, but she nodded, so we went ahead. We prayed together, and she admitted how angry she was at God for the hurts and injustices in her life. Then she laid her anger at the foot of the cross. We asked Jesus to bear it and take it away, so it would no longer stand as a barrier between her and God. Finally, we prayed that God's love would flood her heart as never before.

Our time of prayer was neither dramatic nor emotional, but she took an important step forward that evening. By owning her anger at God, she had begun to disown it. Christ could now bear it in his broken body. As her anger receded, it was replaced by God's love.

Do you need to take a step like that? Pray and invite the Holy Spirit, whom Jesus said will guide us into all truth (John 16:13), to show you if you are angry at God because of past hurts and disappointments in your life. As the Spirit reveals your clenched fists, bring them to the cross. Offer them to the Lord Jesus, and give him permission to turn them into open hands.

Exposed idols. On Palm Sunday the crowds had waved branches and shouted, "Hosanna"; on Good Friday they shook their fists and screamed, "Crucify!" What caused the dramatic 180-degree shift in public opinion? Why did they suddenly turn against Jesus?

"We had thought he was the Messiah who had come to rescue Israel" (Luke 24:21 NLT), two disheartened disciples said to each other on the first Easter as they walked along the road to Emmaus. Their words express their expectation of the Messiah and the expectation of everyone else: that he would be a conquering king, a messiah who would set them free from Rome's tyranny and restore political glory to Israel.

The Palm Sunday parade elevated their hopes. Jesus seemed on the verge of declaring himself king. But he wouldn't conform to their expectations. He insisted on being a suffering servant, definitely *not* what they wanted. What a letdown. By Good Friday their disappointment had turned to contempt and, beyond that, to murderous rage. So their disappointment was the child of their false expectations. And behind it lurked the idol they worshiped: military and political power.

The risen Christ appeared and began walking with the two downcast disciples toward the village of Emmaus. He asked them why they were sad and listened sympathetically as they painfully recounted how the man they thought was the Messiah had been crucified. But then he confronted them, exposing their false expectations: "Oh, how foolish you are, and how slow of heart to believe. . . . Was it not necessary that the Messiah should suffer these things and then enter into his glory?" (Luke 24:25-26).

As we bring our disappointments to the cross, we too may find ourselves being confronted. The suffering Messiah, the one who was crucified, will reveal our false expectations and uncover our idols. It will be painful and unsettling, another blow to an already disappointed heart. We may be tempted to run from it. Instead, walk toward the cross. Invite the confrontation. Let's give the Lord permission to expose our idols, yes, even to destroy them.

"Then their eyes were opened, and they recognized him" (Luke 24:31). Like the two disciples on the road, our moment of recognition will come. Jesus will reveal himself to us, even in the confrontation; he will make his presence known. Then we will find ourselves saying, as they did, "Were not our hearts burning within us while he was talking to us on the road?" (Luke 24:32).

"That same hour they got up and returned to Jerusalem. . . . Then they told what had happened on the road" (Luke 24:33, 35). They had to tell others what the Lord had done. And we will too. At the cross, hearts burdened with disappointment can again become burning hearts. And burning hearts will inevitably become bold ones.

QUESTIONS FOR PERSONAL OR GROUP REFLECTION

1. When have you felt disappointed with God? Has it affected your desire to pray and to attend church? Do you see evidence in your life of "damaged trust receptors" and anger toward God? Does hesitancy to trust in God make it possible for you to relate to the analogy of having one foot on the accelerator while the other is on the brake?

2. "Our disappointments with God are often the children of our false expectations. And behind our false expectations lurk the idols, the gods we worship"(p. 64). What false expectations have you placed on God? What false gods stand behind them? Are you willing to give God permission to expose your idols?

3. Have you ever felt it was wrong or unworthy to express your disappointment with God? In what way does Jesus' cry on the cross "My God, my God, why?" give you permission to express such feelings?

4. "At the foot of the cross, his faith—which endured to the end— can be imparted to us. A wonderful exchange takes place: our damaged trust receptors for his determined faith" (p. 69). Do you need Jesus to impart his faith to you?

5. "Pray and invite the Holy Spirit, whom Jesus said will guide us into all truth (John 16:13), to show you if you are angry at God because of past hurts and disappointments in your life. As the Spirit reveals your clenched fists, bring them to the cross. Offer them to the Lord Jesus, and give him permission to turn them into open hands" (p. 71). What is your response to this courageous prayer and invitation?

5

He Led Captivity Captive

> As he was suspended there, bound hand and foot to the wood
> in apparent weakness, they imagined they had him in their grasp,
> and flung themselves on him with hostile intent. But, far from
> suffering their attack without resistance, he grappled with
> them and mastered them, stripping them of all the armor in which
> they trusted, and held them aloft in his mighty outstretched
> hands, displaying to the universe their helplessness and his own
> unvanquished strength.
>
> F. F. BRUCE

In reflecting on his years of practice as a Christian clinical psychologist, Gary Moon once calculated the number of hours he had spent listening to people. At the time, the total was equivalent to seventeen months of seven-days-a-week, twenty-four-hours-a-day, nonstop counseling. As he considered the myriad of people who had sat in his office, he was struck at first by their incredible diversity. Like their faces, no two person's problems were exactly alike.

Yet as he continued to reflect, Moon was even more impressed by the amazing similarity between his patients, by the common threads running through all of their stories. "I can say with conviction," he writes, "that when I spend a single hour with a client, one of three distinct themes will be evidenced. And in multiple sessions, all three will emerge."[1] He labels these recurring themes "compassion deficits," "behavioral narcotics" and "the two selves."

In the same way a car engine needs oil to run smoothly, human beings need the oil of compassion or unconditional love to operate. Compassion deficits result when that oil is in short supply, especially during our early formative years. Without exception, those who came for counseling quickly led Moon to times and places where they had experienced traumatic compassion deficits. The tragic consequences are "a lifetime of running their 'engines' without enough oil, physical and psychological wear-and-tear, and a deep-seated desire to go home where love can be found."[2]

Compassion deficits can be devastating; not being loved enough damages one's soul. However, unlike car engines, human beings don't usually burn up or shut down when they lack that oil. They somehow keep going. But how do they cope with the pain and emptiness?

By turning to "behavioral narcotics." They rely on them as pain relievers for compassion deficits and anesthetics for a lack of unconditional love. For some, the narcotics are actual chemical substances like drugs or alcohol. But for many, says Moon, the narcotics are not chemical at all but are "patterns and habits of behavior, relating, or coping." He describes some of the more common ones as follows:

- *Habits of workaholism:* filling the mind so full of thoughts, dreams, and activities of success that there is little room left to feel pain caused by irrational, underlying feelings of inadequacy.

- *Habits of control:* constantly striving to maintain control of others, making their will the servants of our own, and binding the hands we secretly fear will strike us.

- *Habits of people pleasing:* constantly monitoring what others expect from us so that we can avoid the pain of their rejection by minimizing its likelihood, becoming in the process slaves of our servanthood.

- *Habits of dependency:* always surrendering our will to the will of another (even to God) for reasons of fear and self-diagnosed inadequacy, instead of enjoying the freedom to follow the advice of love.

- *Habits of perfectionism:* wearing a mask of perfection and rightness to cover inner turmoil and ambiguity.

- *Habits of escape:* taking emotional vacations from pain through the use of alcohol, drugs, or self-destructive patterns of pain-delaying behavior.[3]

Such behavioral narcotics may temporarily deaden the pain of compassion deficits, but they can't provide permanent relief because they don't go to the heart of the problem. As false substitutes, they also keep us from experiencing love and intimacy.

The third shared theme among Moon's patients is the conflict between the two selves. According to Moon, "Sitting in the client's chair, there are always two people and they are battling for occupancy."[4] The false self and the true self vie for the person's throne. The false self wants to remain in control. Its antidote for the agony of compassion deficits is always the same: "Turn to behavioral narcotics you are familiar with, and at all costs, stay in control." The true self, however, desires more. "It wants to restore the rightful order and to assume its proper identity. When the true self reigns, love is king. . . . Its rightful reign is the only true solution to compassion deficits and the substance abuse problem of behavioral narcotics."[5]

Moon's three recurring themes are useful in helping us understand ourselves. The issues we have dealt with so far—rejection, shame and disappointment with God—naturally fall under compassion deficits, since they revolve around thoughts and feelings arising from a lack of unconditional love.

Addictions, the focus of this chapter, fall under Moon's second theme, behavioral narcotics. To numb the pain of compassion deficits and find substitutes for unconditional love, many have fallen into unhealthy behavioral and relational habit patterns like the ones Moon describes. In fact, for scores of people those patterns assume a life of their own. When they become compulsive, unmanageable and out of control, we label them as addictions.

In *Out of the Shadows,* his groundbreaking book on sexual addiction, Patrick Carnes vividly describes the frightening moment when a person finally realizes he or she is a sex addict. Regardless of the nature of one's addiction, his snapshots graphically portray its extreme irrationality:

> When you have to tell yet another lie which you almost believe yourself, . . . when the money you have spent on the last prostitute equals the amount for the new shoes your child needs, . . . when your teenage son finds your pornography, . . . when you see a person on the street you had been sexual with in a restroom, . . . when you make business travel decisions on the basis of the affair you are having, . . . when you leave your job because of a sexual entanglement, . . . when you cringe inside because your friends are laughing at a flasher joke, and you are one.[6]

So many in America today have fallen into such compulsive, unmanageable patterns that addiction has become one of our most pressing and pervasive social problems. Major bookstores often include an entire "Recovery" section related to the subject.

But does the cross have a message for those struggling with addictions?

ADDICTION AND POWERLESSNESS

Experts agree that significant compassion deficits resulting from an unhealthy family life and personal trauma are the root of addiction. Don Crossland spent over twenty years in ministry before he was forced to resign his pastorate when the congregation found out about his sexual addiction. His experience is typical: "As I looked back over the years, I began to realize that I was overtaken in childhood. It was then that seeds of addiction were planted. . . . My childhood was characterized by a lack of emotional openness and human closeness. I was taught . . . that men don't hug, men don't cry, and men don't show their feelings."[7]

For example, Crossland vividly remembers waking up as a young boy during a violent west Texas thunderstorm. Frightened, he ran into his parents' bedroom and crawled in bed next to his father. He immediately woke up and shoved his son onto the floor. Feeling rejected and fearful of the storm, Don began to sob. Then his father berated him for his weakness. "Big boys don't cry," he said angrily.

Don also remembers being molested as a six- and seven-year-old, first by a farm worker and then by one of his father's day laborers. The sexual abuse magnified his shame and his fear of being vulnerable with others.

Like Crossland, most addicts have experienced significant compassion deficits. During childhood their needs for intimacy, identity and adequacy went unmet. In fact, adult addicts have been described as "essentially children hiding out in grown-up bodies, hungrily seeking parents to love them unconditionally."[8]

Out of this addictive root, an addictive mindset develops, revolving around the core beliefs to which addicts usually subscribe:

- I am essentially a bad, worthless person and therefore undeserving of love.

- No one would love me if they really knew me.

- If I don't meet my needs, they will never get met.

All three of these core beliefs directly contradict the Bible's revelation of God's evaluation of us. We are deeply loved by God. When at our worst—hostile, rebellious sinners—God loved us the most. Christ's death on the cross demonstrates our inestimable worth to God and the extent of his love. And Paul boldly affirms in Philippians 4:19, "My God will fully satisfy every need of yours according to his riches in glory in Christ Jesus."

In addition to fostering an addictive mindset, compassion deficits also fuel anger. Stephen Arterburn observes that "addicts are very angry people. Their anger feeds on itself as they reflect endlessly on how they have been hurt and what the world owes them. They cannot relate to others intimately, because their anger blocks their giving of self."[9] Behind the addict's smiling face stands a person who is bitter and judgmental.

Prompted by their core beliefs and fueled by anger over unmet needs, addicts choose to listen to the voice of the false self. No longer do they depend on others to meet their needs, for when they have in the past, they felt powerless and out of control. Instead, they look out for themselves; they seek power and control by taking charge.

Lacking love and intimacy from significant others in their family, addicts turn to substitutes such as drugs, alcohol, spending, gambling, romance, work, food or relationships to dull the pain and fill the void. At first these substitutes seem to work. They offer relief and a pleasurable "high." They reinforce the lie, "I really *don't* need anybody; I can take care of myself. I'm the master of the universe."

Instead of depending on others or God to meet their needs, addicts learn to depend on their substitutes. Having turned to their substitutes for power and control, eventually they become enslaved to them and, ironically, once again stand powerless and out of control.

When does this happen? When does something that might have only functioned as a behavioral narcotic actually become an addic-

tion? In his insightful book *Addiction and Grace,* Gerald May outlines
five characteristics of all addictions.[10] The presence of these characteristics indicates that a behavioral narcotic has become an addiction.

- *Tolerance.* Addicts continually need more of the behavioral
  narcotic to feel satisfied. Their system develops a tolerance for
  the behavior or substance, thus diminishing its desired effect.
  Hence it takes more and more to get the pain relief or the plea-
  sure they need.

- *Withdrawal symptoms.* When addicts are deprived of their behavioral narcotic, their system responds in two ways. First,
  there is a physical and emotional stress reaction as the system
  cries out for the narcotic. Then there is a backlash reaction
  marked by the exact opposite symptoms of those caused by the
  addictive behavioral narcotic itself.

- *Self-deception.* Addicts go to great lengths to justify their behavior and to convince themselves they are still in control. They
  are masters of mental trickery, adept at denial, rationalization
  and various other defense mechanisms.

- *Loss of willpower.* Despite their firm resolutions, addicts can't
  stop the addictive behavior because their will is divided. Although one part sincerely desires to quit, another part tena-
  ciously clings to the addiction. Their determination to quit is
  always short-lived.

- *Distortion of attention.* Addicts become so preoccupied with
  the object of their addiction, they are unable to fix their attention or love on anything else. The particular object has become
  their ultimate concern; it is their god. Idolatry is present in every addiction.

According to May, the litmus test for whether a person suffers from an addiction is the absence of freedom—when addictive desires and behaviors have become habitual and compulsive, enslaving the addict. Their wills are bound. They *cannot* stop. Having exchanged the truth for a lie, they have been given over to their addictive thoughts, their lust and desires, and the idolatry of their false gods (Romans 1:25-28).

Powerless—the word at the heart of the crucial first step of Alcoholics Anonymous' twelve steps—describes the addict best: "We admitted that we were *powerless* over alcohol and that our lives had become unmanageable." By turning away from God and others and turning to substitutes for unconditional love, addicts hope to gain power and control over their lives. Yet in the end they are powerless, slaves to the very substitutes they thought would free them.

THE ALL-POWERFUL ONE BECOMES POWERLESS

In contrast to the addict who grasps for power through some behavioral narcotic, during his final hours Christ the all-powerful One *chose* to become powerless. Jesus declared, "I lay down my life in order to take it up again. No one takes it from me, but I lay it down of my own accord. I have power to lay it down, and I have power to take it up again" (John 10:17-18). In John's account of the story, Jesus was in charge of the situation. Far from being a helpless victim at the mercy of his enemies, he understood exactly what was happening and always remained in control.

For example, when Jesus was taken into custody by those who had come to arrest him, John stresses that *they* didn't seize him. Instead, *he* handed himself over to them.

When Judas and the detachment of soldiers arrived at the Mount of Olives, Jesus stepped forward. "Who are you looking for?" he inquired. When they replied, "Jesus of Nazareth," he declared, "I am he." They took that to mean "I am that man." But throughout John's Gospel, when Jesus said "I am" (8:58), he was calling himself by the name that was used most often in the Old Testament to identify the God of Israel. For instance, when God told Moses to go to Egypt and deliver the Israelites, Moses asked, "Whom shall I say sent me?" God answered, "Say to the Israelites, 'I AM has sent me to you' " (Exodus 3:13-15). Of course, in the garden that night, the Roman soldiers didn't know that in using God's name, Jesus implied his equality with God, but John assumes his readers know.

What happened to the soldiers when Jesus said "I am he" also points toward his identity: they "stepped back and fell to the ground" (John 18:6). In Scripture such a response signals God has appeared on the scene (Ezekiel 1:28; Daniel 2:46; 8:18; Revelation 1:17). The soldiers came in the darkness of night to arrest a common peasant. Instead, they were confronted by a majestic, commanding figure, one who by his words and actions claimed to be God. And that is who he was (and is)—the sovereign, all-powerful One, who choose to become powerless by putting himself in their hands.

In trying to protect Jesus from the soldiers, Peter impulsively resorted to violence. Unsheathing his sword, he slashed off the ear of the high priest's servant. But Jesus would have none of it. He refused to fight power with power, at least not *violent* power. "Put your sword back into its sheath. Am I not to drink the cup that the Father has given me?" he commands Peter (John 18:11). Then, according to Luke's account, Jesus touched the servant's ear and healed him (22:51), his last miracle. From this point on he made no demonstration of power, only ever-increasing powerlessness.

So Jesus *voluntarily* turned himself over to the soldiers. After reaching out his hands to heal the servant, he then offered those same hands to the soldiers as a sign of non-resistance and surrender. Then, says John, they "arrested Jesus and bound him" (18:12). Matthew and Mark both write that later, when the high priest sent Jesus to Pilate, they bound Jesus (Matthew 27:2; Mark 15:1), but only John mentions it happening in the garden.

The Incarnate Word of God through whom all things were made (John 1:3), the all-powerful One whose hands fashioned the stars and planets and flung them into their orbits allowed the soldiers to tie those hands. He stood before them bound, handcuffed as a common criminal. The Author of freedom, the Son who sets us free (John 8:36) surrendered himself and was made captive.

The relinquishing of freedom and power that commences here not only continues during Jesus' final hours, it intensifies. Klaas Schilder delineates three steps in Christ's descending powerlessness. First, at his arrest when he was bound, he was robbed of the power to *act* freely. Second, at the conclusion of his trial, when sentenced to death, he was deprived of his power to *speak* freely. Once the verdict was pronounced, no one listened to him because he was a condemned man. Third, at the cross, where he was mocked and taunted, even his power to *think* freely abandoned him. As the vicious thoughts of others pressed in on him, his mind was too weak to counteract them or form its own thoughts.[11]

What Klaas Schilder analyzed, C. S. Lewis dramatized. In *The Lion, the Witch, and the Wardrobe*, the first of his magical Chronicles of Narnia, is a scene that graphically depicts Christ's voluntary submission and increasing powerlessness. Aslan, the magnificent lion and Christ-figure in the story, willingly turns himself over to the White Witch and her evil horde in a ransom exchange for Edmund, the young boy who had become her prisoner. Lucy and Susan, Edmund's sisters, watch from their hiding place as Aslan surrenders himself. Lewis describes what the girls saw:

A howl and a gibber of dismay went up from the creatures when they first saw the great Lion pacing towards them, and for a moment even the Witch herself seemed to be struck with fear. Then she recovered herself and gave a wild, fierce laugh. "The fool!" she cried. "The fool has come. Bind him fast."

Lucy and Susan held their breaths waiting for Aslan's roar and his spring upon his enemies. But it never came. Four Hags, grinning and leering, yet also (at first) hanging back and half afraid of what they had to do, had approached him. "Bind him, I say!" repeated the White Witch. The Hags made a dart at him and shrieked with triumph when they found that he made no resistance at all. Then others—evil dwarfs and apes—rushed in to help them, and between them they rolled the huge Lion round on his back and tied all his four paws together, shouting and cheering as if they had done something brave, though, had the Lion chosen, one of those paws could have been the death of them all. But he made no noise, even when the enemies, straining and tugging, pulled the cords so tight that they cut into his flesh. Then they began to drag him towards the Stone Table. . . .

He was so huge that even when they got him there it took all their efforts to hoist him onto the surface of it. Then there was more tying and tightening of cords. . . .

When once Aslan had been tied (and tied so that he was really a mass of cords) on the flat stone, a hush fell on the crowd. . . . The Witch bared her arms. . . . Then she began to whet her knife. It looked to the children, when the gleam of the torchlight fell on it, as if the knife were made of stone not steel and it was of a strange and evil shape. . . .

The children did not see the actual moment of the killing. They couldn't bear to look and had covered their eyes.[12]

Of course, Aslan, like Christ, rises in triumph. "There, shining in the sunrise, larger than they had seen him before, shaking his mane (for it had apparently grown again) stood Aslan himself."[13] He comes back to free Edmund and all the creatures from their bondage to the White Witch. Narnia's long winter is finally over, and at last it's springtime. But in order to liberate Narnia, Aslan, like Christ, became a prisoner. He gained power not by asserting it violently but by becoming powerless. He proclaims release to the captives because he himself was made captive.

Earlier, in describing how Christ overcame shame, I highlighted a particular phrase in Colossians 2:15: "And having disarmed the powers and authorities, *he made a public spectacle of them*, triumphing over them by the cross"(NIV, emphasis mine). We saw how through crucifixion, the political and religious leaders intended to make a public spectacle of Jesus but instead, by enduring that shame, he actually made them a public spectacle, shaming them by exposing their true colors. They were not God's allies as they claimed; they were God's adversaries. Otherwise, they would not have crucified the Lord of glory (1 Corinthians 2:8).

But not only did Christ "make a public spectacle" of the powers and authorities, according to Colossians 2:15, he also "disarmed" them and "triumphed" over them on the cross. In some places in the New Testament, the cross is looked on as a defeat that the resurrection turns into a victory (Acts 2:23-36). However, Colossians 2:15 presents the cross itself as a victory.

How can this be? How is this very act of defeat in fact a victory? How does Jesus triumph by becoming powerless? Jesus himself provides the answer.

Prior to his arrest, when he was in the upper room with his disciples, he said, "I will no longer talk much with you, for the ruler of this world is coming. *He has no power over me*; but I do as the Father has commanded me" (John 14:30-31, emphasis mine). The devil and the powers of evil could *never* gain power over him, not even in his death. As a result, he "disarmed" them by taking away their supreme weapon, the power of illusion. For although Satan and the dark powers are a part of creation, they seek to elevate themselves to the place of God the Creator. They claim to be absolute and therefore worthy of worship. Then, through the power of illusion, they seduce us into bowing down to them.

But Jesus refused to become a slave to their illusion. By being obedient even to death, he demonstrated he wasn't bound by them. By voluntarily laying his life down, he proved their claim to power over life and death was false. Thus when Pilate said, "Do you not know that I have power to release you, and power to crucify you?" Jesus immediately corrected him: "You would have no power over me unless it had been given you from above" (John 19:10-11). So he disarmed the powers, stripping away their weapon of illusion.

He also triumphed over the power of evil, winning a great victory by refusing to disobey God, hate his enemies or resort to violence. He overcame not by launching an all-out frontal attack on his adversaries or by beating them at their own game but through the power of suffering love. He chose the way of forgiveness, not retaliation; meekness, not self-assertion. As Peter says, "When he was abused, he did not return abuse; when he suffered, he did not threaten" (1 Peter 2:23). He took everything the powers of evil could throw at him yet remained free, uncontaminated, uncompromised. The devil could gain no hold on him and therefore had to concede defeat.

Christ's resurrection from the dead and his exaltation to God's right hand confirmed and proclaimed the victory he won on the cross. As Peter declared in his Pentecost sermon, "But God raised him up, having freed him from death, because it was impossible for him to be held in its power" (Acts 2:24). Now the tables have been turned. Death is under *his* feet; so are the devil and all dark powers. "When he ascended on high he made captivity itself a captive" (Ephesians 4:8).

KISS YOUR CHAINS!

What does the cross say to those shackled by the chains of addictions?

First, we must admit we are powerless over our addictions. Jesus won victory over sin, death and the devil by becoming powerless. We will never overcome our addiction until we realize and confess we are powerless. We are *not* in control, we are *not* the master of the universe. We can't quit anytime we please. Our willpower is no match for the power of our addictions. The only power we have is the power to admit we are powerless. Only by confessing our absolute weakness will we find strength to overcome.

Pierre D'Harcourt, who was in the French underground during World War II, discovered this principle of power through powerlessness when he was captured by the Nazis. Betrayed and later wounded in a gun battle, he was captured, thrown into a prison cell and handcuffed to the iron frame of the bed. The first hour in his cell was one of the worst in his life. As he lay on his bed feeling utterly alone and hopeless, he turned his face to God and cried out for help.

> Beneath everything, beyond everything, I felt myself humiliated and defeated. I had been so confident, and now my pride had been laid low. There was only one way of coming to terms with my fate if I was not to sink into an abyss of defeatism from which I knew I could never rise again. I must make the gesture of complete humility by offering to God all that I had suffered. I must not only have the courage to accept the suffering He had sent me; I must also thank Him for it, for the opportunity He gave me to find at last His truth and love. I remember the relief of weeping as I realized that this was my salvation
>
> Then the inspiration came to me to kiss the chains which held me prisoner, and with much difficulty I at last managed to do this. I am not a credulous person, but . . . there can be no doubt in my mind that some great power from outside momentarily entered into me. Once my lips had touched the steel I was freed from the terror that possessed me. As the handcuffs had brought the terror of death to me, now by kissing my manacles I had turned them from bonds into a key. . . . In the blackness of that night my faith gave me light. Peace returned to me and I slept quietly, accepting death which would bring me life.[14]

To be set free from the bondage of addiction, we too must discover this liberating principle. Instead of fighting the chains of our addictions, let's kiss them and acknowledge our powerlessness. We cannot deny or despair over it but must rather embrace it. Our honest acceptance is the first gigantic step on the path to freedom.

Second, in our powerlessness we must cry out to Jesus, for his strength is made perfect in our weakness (2 Corinthians 12:9). Our powerlessness releases his power. Because he became powerless, he is not only a higher power but has been exalted by God to the place of highest power (Philippians 2:9). For "God's weakness is stronger than human strength" (1 Corinthians 1:25). All power and authority has been given to him. That power, the very power that raised Christ from the dead, can be imparted to us (Ephesians 1:19-20). The Lord can break the chains of our addictions. So we must call on him to deliver us and give him permission to do anything necessary to set us free.

Third, in our powerlessness we must reach out to others for help. Make no mistake, achieving freedom from addiction will involve a long, difficult process. To break an addictive behavior cycle alone is a major accomplishment, but that is only the tip of the iceberg. We still must deal with an addictive mindset (the lies we have believed about ourselves) and an addictive root (our wounds and compassion deficits). Most addicts have no idea how much internal change is necessary before they can walk in long-term freedom. As Ted Roberts explains, "This depth of change doesn't come in a moment. It usually takes three to five years to go through the process, with God working miracles every step of the way. The goal isn't just to get the noose off the soul, but to become someone who is experiencing all that God has for him."[15] A determined personal commitment to change coupled with involvement with others in a twelve-step program or a recovery support group, individual counseling and spiritual disciplines (such as worship, Bible study, prayer, participation in a small group, involvement in Christian service) are necessary to reach that goal.

But that goal is possible through Christ, the one who accepted weakness and powerlessness in order to become the power of God for us. His grace is sufficient each step of the way. Because he became a slave, he can now proclaim release to the captives and freedom for those who are bound (Luke 4:18).

Let us then confess our powerlessness and rely on him each step on the way to freedom. May the hymn writer's words be our constant prayer: "Nothing in my hand I bring; Simply to Thy cross I cling."[16]

QUESTIONS FOR PERSONAL OR GROUP REFLECTION

1. What early memories do you associate with the term "compassion deficits"? What feelings accompany these memories?

2. Have you ever turned to behavioral narcotics to numb the pain of a compassion deficit? Which particular patterns of behavior have held the greatest draw for you: workaholism? control? people pleasing? dependency? perfectionism? escape? How have these false substitutes for unconditional love kept you from experiencing genuine love and intimacy?

3. While compassion deficits form the emotional root of addiction, faulty core beliefs shape the addict's mindset (pp. 78-79). Have any of these lies seemed true to you? Based on Scripture, what truths about you need to replace these lies? Do you need to ask the Lord Jesus to impart the knowledge of those truths into the depths of your being?

4. "By turning away from God and others and turning to substitutes for unconditional love, addicts hope to gain power and control over their lives. Yet in the end they are powerless, slaves to the very substitutes they thought would free them" (p. 81). Have you found

yourself in such a powerless position—needing healing from compassion deficits and forgiveness for turning to an addictive idol? Do you need to ask the Lord, who voluntarily became powerless, to break that addiction's power in your life?

5. Have you heard recovering addicts tell the story of how their lives were transformed following the admission of powerlessness over their substance of choice? In sharing their prevailing "experience, strength and hope," they, like Jesus, make a "public spectacle" of the power that wanted to destroy them. Of Jesus it is said, "When he ascended on high he made captivity itself a captive." How do you see the fruit of this victory unfolding in your own life?

6. As we walk the road toward freedom, we must (1) acknowledge our powerlessness, (2) cry out to Jesus and (3) reach out to others for help (pp. 86-89). Which of these liberating steps is Christ asking you to take at this time?

6

Deliverance for Those
Who Are Bound

*When Satan attacks you, command him in the name of Jesus
to bend his neck. On the back of it you'll find there's a nail-scarred
footprint!*

E. STANLEY JONES

If I could just count to three," Bill said dejectedly. "But before I
can even get that far, it's as if something takes over and I explode
with rage."

I had first become acquainted with Bill ten years earlier when he
was attending seminary. He had been a top-notch student, excelling
in several of my advanced theology classes. Now Bill was an experienced pastor back on campus pursuing a doctor of ministry degree.
In a few months, he would begin planting a new church in a growing suburb, an assignment given to him by his denomination.

"I believe God is calling me to plant this church," he said confi-
dently. "But I'm also afraid I'm not spiritually fit. In growing a congregation, I know there'll be times when conflict arises. I'll also be
in chaotic situations where I feel out of control. How will I react
then? Often when things like that have happened in my marriage relationships, my anger has erupted and all hell has broken loose."

Bill's first marriage had ended in divorce, and his uncontrollable anger had been a major contributing factor in its breakdown. He had recently remarried, but the pattern had continued. "Three times in the last month, I've raged at Diane," he confessed sadly. "We deeply love each other, and she has been very patient with me. But I'm afraid if I don't stop, my raging will eventually destroy this marriage too."

Bill had come to me because he knew I believed in the reality of the demonic and the possibility that committed Christians could be "demonized" (under the control or influence of demons in certain areas of their lives). "I have to admit I've been skeptical about anything like that," he said. "But when I fly into a rage, sometimes there is such an 'otherness' about it that is so alien to who I am in Christ, I have begun to wonder whether some of this might be the result of direct demonic influence."

Sensing that Bill might be on the right track, I began explaining demonization to him. "Imagine your anger is like a fire. Through the power of the Holy Spirit, you are seeking to keep it under Christ's lordship and control. But what if in certain anger-provoking situations, while you're trying to control the rising flames, someone is simultaneously pouring gasoline on the fire? How can you possibly keep it from raging out of control?

"Under certain conditions, having gained an entry point in our lives, demons can work like that. They act as hypercatalysts, piggybacking on existing problems so that at times our behavior seems almost compulsive. Our willpower simply isn't strong enough to withstand their onslaughts. For Christians who are demonized, in certain areas of their lives the playing field, instead of being level, is such a steep uphill incline it's almost impossible for them to run the race for Christ victoriously.

"Does this mean that demonized persons are not responsible for their behavior? Like the comedian Flip Wilson, can they excuse themselves, insisting that 'the devil made me do it'? By no means. For as significant as demonic influence may be, it is *never* the primary issue in someone's life. It may be a deadly, destructive consequence or fruit, but it is not the root problem. Charles Kraft has a helpful analogy. He says demons are like rats, which are attracted to garbage.[1] The main problem is the garbage, consisting of things like our persistent sinful behaviors, our reactions to our emotional wounds, and sinful generational influences and patterns. These are issues for which we are responsible. When we deal with them, when we get rid of the garbage, then the rats won't have anything to feed on, and it's easy to make them go away."

What I said made sense to Bill. Before dealing with the demonic—whether it was directly involved or not—we needed to consider the garbage in his life. So we began to explore that.

On numerous occasions as a young boy, he had been deeply wounded by his father's violent temper. The chaos created by his father's explosive anger created a sense of fear and helplessness in Bill. The experience of being shamed and humiliated by his father also fueled his own anger. Often he would suppress it; sometimes he would vent it on his younger brother. There also seemed to be a generational pattern at work since, by all accounts, his grandfather was also a very angry man.

Bill's two most persistent sins were explosive anger and sexual lust. In chaotic situations when he felt out of control, he would erupt like a volcano. But rather than depleting his anger, venting it on those around him only increased it. Giving in to lust also became a way of dealing with chaos. At times he had turned to fantasy, masturbation, pornography or promiscuity for comfort. However, instead of bringing relief, anger and lust only led to guilt and depression which, in turn, caused pain and chaos, thus fueling the cycle all over again.

Bill was acutely aware of the emotional dynamics involved in his sinful behaviors. He had previously gained significant self-awareness

through the help of several Christian counselors. They had helped
him understand the childhood roots of his anger and had also introduced him to anger management techniques. He was still a slave to
his anger—otherwise he wouldn't have been in my office—but I was
thankful for the foundations of freedom already in place in his life.
Thanks to his previous counselors, we didn't have to lay those foundations, something that would have taken considerable time. We
could build on what was already there.

There was one other type of sin I probed Bill about: his involvement, either knowingly or unknowingly, in any occult activities. I explained that such involvement, which is clearly forbidden by Scripture (Deuteronomy 18:9-13), often opens the door to significant
demonic influence. This turned out to be a minor area of concern,
although Bill did recall that on one occasion as a child he had innocently played with a ouija board, and on another, had participated
in a séance.

Having sufficiently discussed the issues which may have been creating opportunities for direct demonic influence in his life, we then
entered into an intense period of prayer where we brought his spiritual and emotional garbage to the cross of Christ. Bill repented of
and renounced his turning to anger and rage as a friend to help him
deal with problems, his participation in various forms of lust, his resentment toward his father and grandfather, and his participation in
all occult activities, innocent or not.

I reminded him of 1 Peter 1:18-19: "You know that you were ransomed from the futile ways inherited from your ancestors, not with
perishable things like silver or gold, but with the precious blood of
Christ, like that of a lamb without defect or blemish." On the basis
of that verse we cancelled any generational bond of anger between
Bill, his father and his grandfather. Next we turned to 1 John 1:7-9,
which states that "the blood of Jesus his Son cleanses us from all sin"
and "If we confess our sins, he who is faithful and just will forgive us

our sins and cleanse us from all unrighteousness." On the basis of those verses, we then declared that Bill was forgiven and cleansed. His sins had been nailed to Christ's cross and could no longer be held against him; the garbage associated with these things was gone. There was therefore nothing left for any demonic rats—if they were there—to cling to or feed on.

Finally, with Bill's permission and with the authority of Christ, I directly confronted any demons that might have gained influence in his life through the garbage that had been there. Almost immediately Bill reported that he saw strobe lights flashing in his closed eyes, and he could not stop them from twitching. Tears began to flow down his cheeks, but he was *not* crying.

It was obvious that something other than Bill was present. Several demonic spirits were in fact at work. After they had been identified and it was established that they no longer had any right to be there— all that had been taken away through Christ's cross—I commanded the demons to leave, and they soon did.

As Bill and I rejoiced over what Jesus had done, I invited the Holy Spirit to fill him anew and afresh. In those areas of his life where there had been demonic influence, we asked the Spirit to take control. Before he left my office, I instructed him to keep short accounts with God, particularly if he gave in to anger or lust. I also encouraged him to keep moving toward emotional wholeness. Finally, we discussed how he needed to abide in Christ through regular times of prayer and Scripture reading if he expected to walk in victory.

That particular day marked a crucial turning point in Bill's life. In an e-mail I received from him almost five years later, he said, "I am happy to report that since our time together I have never lost my temper again. Of course, I have gotten angry from time to time, but never anything approaching my rage of the past. The playing field truly was leveled, and I have had peace and victory since that day, praise the Lord!"

THE DEMONIZATION OF CHRISTIANS

Demonization like Bill experienced is yet another damaging effect of human hurts.

At first I was reticent to include a chapter on this subject. Because of its controversial nature and proneness to misunderstanding, I shied away from it. But after further reflection and prayer, and in the light of continued ministry experiences with committed Christians like Bill who are in bondage in certain areas of their lives, I became convinced that it needed to be included.

Of course, most emotional hurts do *not* result in demonization. The effects we have discussed in previous chapters are much more likely to result from emotional wounds than demonization. Demonization is the exception, not the rule, so we should never immediately assume there's a demon lurking behind every area of brokenness or bondage in our lives. Instead, we should generally consider the possibility of demonization only after we've explored other possible spiritual, psychological and even physiological causes.

Nevertheless, there are a significant number of Christians like Bill who have diligently sought help and have explored the various causes, yet continue to live in defeat and bondage. I agree with Terry Wardle, a counselor and professor of spiritual formation: "I do not believe demons lurk behind every bush. But I do believe that a level of demonization can be at least a contributing factor and under some circumstances the primary cause of the problems some people face."[2]

Among evangelical Christians there is broad consensus that Satan uses demons to tempt and attack believers. But generally such demonic activities have been considered external in nature. Demons, then, exert pressure on us from the outside, in much the same way other human persons might seek to influence us to do something. They might make suggestions to us, plant thoughts in our minds, entice us or play on our fears and weaknesses. However, such "demonic influence" or "demonic oppression" (phrases that are commonly used to describe such demonic activity) is always from the outside and therefore limited.

But can demonic activity go beyond this? Can demons also exert internal and therefore more direct influence on believers? Can a Christian be *demonized*, that is, inhabited or controlled by a demon? Since the 1970s a growing number of pastors, counselors, teachers, theologians and Bible scholars in North America and Europe have said yes.[3] Based on my study of Scripture and church history, and my experiences in ministry, I find myself in agreement with them.

For many Christians, however, to suggest that demonization is a possibility immediately raises a number of questions. The two most frequently asked are (1) Doesn't the idea of internal demonic control or influence imply that the believer is demon-possessed? and (2) How can a Christian who is indwelt by Christ (Colossians 1:27) and a temple of the Holy Spirit (1 Corinthians 6:19) also be inhabited by demons?

In response to the first question, those who affirm the possibility of demonization insist that the two should not be equated. The word *possession* implies lawful ownership and absolute control over something or someone. As Clinton Arnold writes, "To be possessed by the devil is to be owned by the devil and to be totally under his control. It means that the person is incapacitated and no longer able to act on the basis of his or her own volition."[4] Understood in that way, it is impossible for committed Christians to be demon-possessed. Jesus is their Lord and rightful owner. They belong to him and therefore are his possession.

Much of the confusion over this issue stems from an unfortunate translation in the King James Version of the Bible. The KJV translators rendered the Greek verb *daimonizomai* as "demon-possessed" or "possessed by a demon" even though the idea of possession isn't inherent in the word. When they rendered the Greek noun *daimon*, they simply transliterated it. That's how we got our

English word "demon." If they had simply transliterated *daimoni-zomai*, they would have rendered it "demonize" or "to be demon-ized." The word's essential meaning is "to subject or be subject to demonic influence."

Not only does the word *possession* stem from a poor translation of the Greek, it is an all-or-nothing word implying total ownership and control. *Demonization* is a better choice because it is both more ac-curate and more compatible with the varying degrees of internal control that demons may exert on persons. It's also a word that can be used to describe genuine Christians. There is no question that Jesus Christ is their Lord and Savior and that they thus belong to him. But they still may be described as demonized because in cer-tain areas of their lives, demons continue to exert a significant mea-sure of internal control. Think of it like the criminal influence in a city. Even though the center of the city and city hall are free and un-der government control, some of the back alleys and side streets may still be controlled by criminals.

This brings us to the second question: How can demons inhabit Christians when Christ dwells in them? If our body is a temple of the Holy Spirit, how can an evil spirit also inhabit our body?

Such either-or thinking is based on the law of physics that two ob-jects cannot occupy the same space at the same time. The problem with applying a physics law to spiritual matters, however, is that spir-its don't occupy space the way material bodies do. Space contains bodies, not spirits. Even the distinction I've made between spirits be-ing located internally or externally, inside or outside the person, must not be pressed too far.

Much of the spatial language in Scripture used to describe spiri-tual realities is metaphorical and must not be taken too literally. Often the authors of Scripture are seeking to convey the idea of au-thority and control. To be "spirit-filled, " for example, is not prima-rily about space—like filling up a cup with water. We can easily be misled when we conceive of it in that way. Rather, it's about being totally yielded and under the control of the Spirit. So in Ephesians 5:18, Paul contrasts being drunk with wine (under the control or influence of alcohol) with being filled with the Spirit (under the control or influence of the Holy Spirit). To be Spirit-filled, then, is to be Spirit-controlled and therefore Christ-controlled.

Scripture also indicates that there are degrees of yieldedness to the control of the Holy Spirit. For example, Paul describes some of the Christians at Corinth as being "of the flesh, and behaving according to human inclinations" (1 Corinthians 3:3). Although they were believers in Christ, they were still controlled in some areas by the desires of the flesh. Might not the same be said of some Christians with regard to demons? Just as the flesh continues to exert control over certain areas of their lives, so might demons to the extent that it would be appropriate to describe them as demonized.

I wish I understood more about the spiritual realm. I do know that when a person becomes a Christian they are transferred from the kingdom of darkness into the kingdom of light, from the domain of the prince of this world to the domain of the Prince of Peace. In Christ they are a new creation (2 Corinthians 5:17) and under new management. I also believe that generally at conversion or baptism there is an invasion of the Holy Spirit that breaks most of us free from any direct internal demonic attachment.

Yet in the actual experience of some Christians, such is not always the case. Because of certain unresolved spiritual and emotional issues in their lives, demons are able to maintain an internal grip on them in some areas; they aren't automatically expelled. And unless their presence is acknowledged and dealt with, they can continue to wreak havoc in the believer's life.

Terry Wardle offers a helpful summary. He suggests that demonized persons experience demonic activity in four primary ways: harassment, oppression, affliction and bondage. There is also progression in moving from one type of demonic activity to the next, indicating a deeper level of control or influence. Here is how he briefly describes each:

Harassment. Much the same as a hornet flies around a person's head, annoying and distracting him, so it can be with this level of demonization. The demon does not keep the person away from his or her appointed course, but does seek to bother and discourage him.

Oppression. This level of demonic activity is much like a fog that settles in upon a person. The individual finds it more difficult to stay on track, and often battles varying levels of emotional and spiritual oppression. It can be more difficult for a person to keep focused on what is true and right.

Affliction. Jesus often cast out demons when people suffered from physical sickness. At this level of activity, demons seek to bring emotional, spiritual and physical suffering to a person in an effort to defeat and demoralize them.

Bondage. The demon spirit is exercising a certain level of control in an area of a person's life. This demonization is possible because of personal choices that give room for this type of bondage. Despite personal efforts to move beyond the problem of sinful behavior, the individual finds it difficult to resist, and repeatedly fails to find freedom.[5]

In cases of demonization, the redemption and victory that was accomplished and won through Christ's death on the cross must be applied to the particular areas where the person is experiencing these types of demonic activity. Through forgiveness, healing and deliverance, the spiritual and emotional garbage must be dealt with and the demons cast out; otherwise, the person will continue to experience defeat.

NAILED TO THE CROSS

Jesus came preaching freedom to the captives and deliverance for those who are bound (Luke 4:18-19). "By the finger of God" he cast out demons as a sign that the kingdom of God had come (Luke 11:20), and he gave his followers authority to do likewise in his name (Matthew 10:8; Luke 10:17-20). He came to attack the strongman Satan, overpower him, take away the armor in which he trusted and divide his plunder (Luke 11:22). All throughout his ministry, Jesus was engaged in warfare and combat with Satan. John tells us that this was the reason the Son of God came: "to destroy the works of the devil"(1 John 3:8). Every time he healed the sick, drove out demons or exercised his lordship over disordered nature, Jesus won a battle in the war against the evil one.

But there was a climactic battle, a turning point in the war, where Jesus inflicted a mortal wound on Satan. That battle was fought and won on the cross where the serpent Satan's head was crushed (Genesis 3:15), and his ultimate fate was sealed. Through his death on the cross, he "destroy[ed] the one who had the power of death, that is, the devil, and free[d] those who all their lives were held in slavery by the fear of death" (Hebrews 2:14-15).

Yet how was the devil defeated on Calvary? How did Jesus win this great battle with Satan? In the previous chapter, we discovered part of the answer when we explained how, according to Colossians 2:15, through his obedience to the point of death Christ "disarmed" the dark powers and "triumphed" over them. In freely choosing to lay down his life in obedience to the Father, he demonstrated he wasn't bound by them and proved their claim to have power over life and death was false. Because of his unswerving obedience, he also refused to turn away from God, hate his enemies or resort to violence against them. Because Jesus remained free, uncontaminated and uncompromised, the devil could gain no hold on him and finally had to concede defeat.

On the cross, Jesus also dealt with Satan's hold on all of humanity as well, an aspect of Christ's triumph that is particularly significant for the problem of demonization. The apostle Paul graphically describes Christ's victory in Colossians 2:13-15: "God made you alive together with him [Christ], when he forgave us all our trespasses, erasing the record that stood against us with its legal demands. He set this aside, nailing it to the cross. He disarmed the rulers and authorities and made a public example of them, triumphing over them in it."

Notice how the victory Christ won over the powers of evil is bound up here with what Christ did in forgiving our sins. In fact, the relationship between the two seems to be one of cause and effect. Forgiveness is the foundation on which freedom is built. Commenting on this passage, New Testament scholar Eduard Lohse says, "On the cross of Christ the certificate of indebtedness is erased; on the cross of Christ the powers and principalities are disempowered. Consequently, where there is forgiveness of sins, there is freedom from the 'powers' and 'principalities', there is life and salvation."[6]

How then did Jesus win the decisive battle against Satan and his evil principalities? Not by overcoming power with power through a direct, violent encounter with the prince of darkness. Jesus did sometimes use that approach in casting out demons during his earthly ministry, but not in his confrontation with evil at the cross. The battle Jesus and Satan fought there wasn't like the clash of two titans locked in a mortal struggle to the death. Instead, Jesus won the battle by erasing the record that stood against us and satisfying its legal demands. Augustine said it well: "It pleased God that for the sake of rescuing men from the power of the devil, the devil should be overcome not by power but by justice."[7]

In describing how Jesus overcame the devil by justice, Paul refers to the ancient custom of canceling debts. The Greek word he uses for the "record" that stood against us is *cheirographon* and has been defined as "a hand-written document, specifically a certificate of indebtedness, a bond."[8] Owing our life and existence to God, we are under obligation to keep his law. But because of our sinfulness, all of us have failed miserably. So the record with its legal demands signifies our giant IOU for sin, the huge debt we all owe but can never repay.

However, through his sacrificial death on the cross, Jesus dealt with that record and paid our debt in full. Paul uses three verbs to describe how Christ accomplished this. He "erased" the record (the Greek word *exaleipsas* literally means he wiped the slate clean), he "set it aside," and he "nailed it to the cross."

Some New Testament scholars see in the record that was nailed to the cross an allusion to the *titulus,* the wooden tablet on which the crucified person's crimes were recorded. The Romans often nailed it over the crucified person's head so that the public would know why he or she had been executed. On the *titulus* over Jesus, Pilate ordered it should simply read "the King of the Jews" (John 19:19-22). According to Colossians 2:14, if Paul had ordered the inscription it would have read "the King who died—not for his own sins but for the sins of others." That may be pressing the metaphor too far, but with Peter O'Brien we can say this much for sure: "This is a vivid way of saying that because Christ has been nailed to the cross our debt has been completely forgiven."[9]

Through his death, then, Jesus has stamped "Paid in full" on the record that stood against us. He has declared it null and void. There is a verse in the popular hymn "It is Well with My Soul" that expresses it powerfully:

> My sin, oh, the bliss of this glorious thought!
> My sin, not in part but the whole,
> Is nailed to the cross, and I bear it no more,
> Praise the Lord, praise the Lord, O my soul!

And because it has been nailed to the cross, the devil now has no rightful claim on us. The Accuser—for that's what Satan's name means—no longer has any legal accusation to bring against us. Thus we have been set free from our slavery to Satan and all his demonic powers.

Jesus won the decisive battle in the war not through a direct frontal attack on the evil one but by removing his right to hold us in his power. Through the just payment of our debts, he has taken away every legal claim that the evil powers had on us. By liberating us from sin, he has also liberated us from Satan.

However, the first liberation, the liberation from sin, is primary. That's why "Christ died for our sins" (1 Corinthians 15:3; cf. 1 Peter 3:18) is the dominant note in the New Testament understanding of the cross. But as a consequence of that primary liberation, a significant secondary liberation—from Satan and all his demonic powers—has also occurred.

Understanding this truth is crucial; otherwise we may end up giving Satan more power and authority than is actually his. For although the New Testament clearly teaches that human beings have become victims and prisoners of Satan, it never attributes our enslavement to some inherent power or rightful dominion he has over us. Our captivity is a consequence of our own rebellion, for which we ourselves are responsible. Beginning with Adam, all have sinned and, as a result, have lost control of what should have been under our dominion and have fallen under the control of demonic powers. The devil gained power over Adam and Eve by enticing them to disobey God. By their own disobedient choice they gave themselves over to his control. He wasn't able to simply impose his control over them. As a creature subject to God's sovereignty and limitations, Satan never had an inherent right to do that. He could only gain that right if we, by choosing to act independently of God, gave it to him. And unfortunately, we did.

But in rescuing us from Satan's dominion over us, Jesus didn't attack him directly. If he had, he would have given the devil more due than he deserved. Instead, Jesus dealt with our sin and rebellion. As the writer of Hebrews states, "He has appeared once for all at the end of the age to remove sin by the sacrifice of himself" (9:26). For by removing sin, he also removed the right the devil had to hold us captive.

DELIVERANCE FROM DEMONIZATION

Christ won the victory over the devil by nailing our sin to the cross, and in doing so, he established a sure foundation of freedom from demonic captivity. Michael Green summarizes: "Christ is the conqueror over all the power of the Enemy, and on the cross he inflicted such a crushing defeat on the devil that whenever his name is named in faith, Satan is bound to flee. . . . The demons have to leave when commanded to do so in the name of the Victor."[10] Green says he has seen this happen time and time again when ministering to those afflicted by demons, and that has been my experience as well. Demons shudder at the mention of Christ's name and especially at the mention of his blood. Like Satan, they are overcome, as John the apostle declares in his vision:

> by the blood of the Lamb
> and by the word of [our] testimony. (Revelation 12:11)

However, Christ's blood must be applied to be effective in our lives. On the night of the first Passover in Egypt, it wasn't enough for a Hebrew family simply to slay a lamb as God had commanded (Exodus 12:6). They were also instructed to take the blood of the slain lamb and smear it on the doorpost of their house (Exodus 12:21-23). Only then would they be protected from the destroyer and set free from slavery. In the same way, it is not enough for Christ to have shed his blood on Calvary. The benefits of his death—forgiveness and freedom—must be personally received and appropriated. His blood must be applied—sprinkled on the doorpost of our hearts and in every chamber as well.

Demonization occurs in Christians when there are certain areas in their life where Christ's blood has not been appropriated. Let me emphasize that it's not because they aren't truly committed Christians. They have received Christ as Savior and Lord and are sincerely seeking to follow after him. But they are demonized (not demon-possessed) in the sense that demons still maintain a significant level of control or influence in specific areas of their lives.

How then are they to be set free from demonic harassment, oppression, affliction and bondage? How are they to gain victory over the powers of darkness? Jesus' victory at the cross provides the pattern. Instead of engaging in a direct cosmic struggle with the prince of darkness, he removed the basis for Satan's dominion over us by taking our sin and nailing it to the cross, canceling our debt and wiping our slate clean. In finding freedom from demonization, that should be our focus too—not demons themselves but the basis for their dominion in our lives.

Sometimes well-meaning Christians involved in deliverance ministry will immediately attempt to engage in a direct frontal attack on demons. So they shout and rail at demons and resort to various other commando tactics. This "Rambo" approach to deliverance gives the demonic more due than it deserves.

Make no mistake, there is a legitimate time and place for direct confrontation, a time when, in Jesus' name, we take the authority he has given us and command demons to leave. But that should not be our primary focus. As I said to Bill, "The main problem is not the demonic rats but the garbage consisting of things like our persistent sinful behaviors, our sinful reactions to our emotional wounds, and sinful generational influences and patterns. When we take responsibility and deal with these issues, when we get rid of the garbage, the rats won't have anything to feed on, and it's easy to get rid of them."

Our focus, then, should be on the spiritual and emotional garbage—the basis for demonic influence and control—not on the demons themselves. That is how Christ won the victory over the darkness; that is how his victory is worked out in our lives too.

Several years ago, as I was reading a contemporary paraphrase of *The Little Flowers of St. Francis*, I came across a wonderful illustration of this principle. This delightful spiritual classic is composed of "little flowers," vignettes about Francis of Assisi and his friars, which were compiled about a hundred years after his death. As I read "St. Francis and the Angry Friar," I realized that for centuries wise Christians have rightly understood where our focus should be when dealing with demons. Here then is this "little flower":

One day at prayer in the friary at Portiuncula,
St. Francis saw
    (by divine revelation)
    the friary surrounded and attacked
    by an army of devils.

        Not one devil could enter;
        the friars lived holy lives, and the
        devils therefore found no place to enter.
        Yet they persisted.

            One friar got angry at another,
            and privately thought about accusing him
            to take revenge.

            This opened the door and
            a devil came into the friary
            to cling to the angry brother.

Well! Francis, guarding shepherd of the flock,
called in the angry friar
so the wolf wouldn't eat the lamb.

Francis ordered the friar to
cough up the poison in his soul
(the anger against his brother)
which allowed the devil to come in.

Horror gripped the friar! (Francis saw through him!)
He confessed his sin;
He acknowledged his fault.
He humbly requested mercy and penance.

The sin forgiven and penance granted,
the devil made tracks and left him.
Naturally the brother thanked God,
for his shepherd had helped him get free.

He returned to the others.
the spiritual surgery successful.
and decidedly grew in holiness.

In praise of Christ. Amen."

Francis was a wise shepherd of the flock. When he saw a demon clinging to an angry brother, he didn't confront the *demon*, he confronted the *brother* about the issue that opened the door for the demon—"the poison in his soul," his anger and unforgiveness. Francis admonished the friar to deal with that, to "cough up" the poison. When he confessed his sin and received forgiveness, the demon had nothing to cling to and "made tracks and left him."

Of course, in some cases demonization is much more complicated. Attaining full freedom may involve a long, drawn-out process. But the basic principle always holds true: take away the garbage; deal with the areas of sin and brokenness in your life. Bring the power of the cross to bear upon those areas. Experience the forgiving, cleansing and healing power of Christ's blood. Make that the focus and freedom will follow.

Could there be an area of your life where you are experiencing demonization? As I said, I hesitated to include this chapter partly because I was concerned that some readers would immediately jump to that conclusion. So please don't. Before you conclude anything, pray and ask the Holy Spirit to guide you into all truth. Then sit down and talk with someone like a wise pastor, an experienced counselor, spiritual director or someone who specializes in healing prayer. Persons like these can help you discern if there is a significant demonic component to your problem or whether it is only spiritual, psychological or physiological in nature. They can also help set you free from direct demonic influence if that is necessary.

Above all, continue to work on the spiritual and emotional garbage in your life. Whether there is a significant demonic component or not, keep seeking forgiveness and release from your sins and healing for your wounds. Walk in the light of God's truth. Let it penetrate your innermost self. Bring your garbage to the cross. As it is cleansed and transformed through the power of his blood, the things to which the demonic might cling will be taken away. When that happens, freedom from sin and, if necessary, freedom from demonization, are sure to follow.

QUESTIONS FOR PERSONAL OR GROUP REFLECTION

1. Before reading this chapter, how would you have defined *demonization*? After reading this chapter, can you differentiate "demonization" from terms such as "demonic oppression" and "demonic possession"? Had you considered the role that demons might play in modern times?

2. If demons are like rats that are attracted to the garbage of our persistent sinful behaviors, our reactions to our emotional wounds, and sinful generational influences and patterns, how might we keep our souls "clean" and beyond the scope of demonic influence?

3. While genuine Christians belong to Jesus Christ, they may still experience various forms of demonic influence such as harassment, oppression, affliction and bondage. In what area of your life do you feel most susceptible to demonic influence?

4. Jesus erased the record that stood against us and satisfied its legal demands. He paid our debt in full. By liberating us from sin, Jesus also liberated us from Satan. When we allow Jesus himself to sweep away the garbage in our souls, demonic "rats" don't have anything to feed on. Is there lingering "garbage" in your life that you need to invite Jesus to sweep away?

5. What prevents you from bringing the garbage to the cross? Ignorance? Shame? Unbelief? Impatience? Feelings of defeat? What lies are you believing that continue to allow demonic influence in your life?

Part Two

THE CROSS AND THE

PATH TO HEALING

7

Embracing the Pain

We are healed of a suffering only by experiencing it to the full.

MARCEL PROUST

When I picture the cross," writes Andrea Midgett, "always, always, I see arms. The outstretched arms of Jesus." If he had been stoned like Stephen, she points out, Jesus would have automatically held them up to protect his face. If he had been beheaded like his cousin John the Baptist, they would have been tied behind his back. "Instead, Jesus' arms were stretched taut, leaving bare his heart. Even when he could no longer physically hold them out, his arms were held in place by the nails."[1]

As we have considered rejection, shame, disappointment with God, addiction and demonization, we have seen how the cross powerfully addresses the destructive effects of human hurts. But the cross also reveals much about the process of healing. The extended arms of Jesus on the cross illustrate the crucial first step in the healing process: Jesus opens himself to the excruciating pain. He makes himself vulnerable. He holds nothing back. With his exposed heart and pain-racked body, Jesus embraces the agony of the cross. His outspread arms teach us that healing happens not by avoiding suffering but by accepting and actively bearing it. Those on the healing path must be willing to walk into and through—not away from or around—pain.

Throughout his ministry, Jesus was tempted to divert from this path. "If you are the Son of God," the devil whispered to him in the wilderness, "turn stones into bread. . . . Throw yourself down from the temple" (Matthew 4:1-11). The tempter urged Jesus to prove he was the Son of God by exercising his rights and privileges. Knowing he couldn't deter Jesus from doing God's will, Satan tempted him to do it his own way or the people's way rather than God's way.

Earlier when he was baptized, Jesus, the sinless one, willingly assumed the role of a suffering servant by identifying himself with sinners. His father's voice from heaven, "This is my Son, the Beloved, with whom I am well pleased" (Matthew 3:17), affirmed the path he had chosen. But that was before his forty days alone in the wilderness. Worn out by the scorching heat, weak from his long fast, subjected to Satan's subtle schemes, what would he do now? Would he remain on the path of self-denial and suffering?

"Away with you, Satan, for it is written,
  'Worship the Lord your God,
    and serve only him.' " (Matthew 4:10)

Jesus rebuked the tempter, refusing to be diverted from doing God's will God's way. So the devil left him "until an opportune time" (Luke 4:13).

Such a time came when Jesus first told his disciples he would "undergo great suffering" and even be killed, only to rise again three days later (Matthew 16:21). Moments before Jesus' prediction, when Peter declared Jesus was the Messiah, Jesus blessed and affirmed him. But after Jesus declared he would suffer and die, Peter "took him aside and began to rebuke him, saying, 'God forbid it, Lord! This must never happen to you' " (Matthew 16:22). Peter thought it ludicrous that any such thing could happen to the Messiah. He would conquer Israel's enemies, not suffer at their hands.

But in a flash Jesus turned on Peter. "Get behind me, Satan! You are a stumbling block to me; for you are setting your mind not on divine things but on human things" (Matthew 16:23). Peter's bold declaration that Jesus was the long-awaited Messiah came from heaven, but his adamant refusal to accept Jesus' prediction of his suffering and death came straight from hell. Perceiving him to be Satan's mouthpiece, Jesus sternly rebuked Peter and reiterated his commitment to God's ordained path.

When the time came for him to walk that path, he agonized in the Garden of Gethsemane to the point that his sweat became like great drops of blood (Luke 22:44). "Father, if you are willing, remove this cup from me," was his desperate cry. Everything within him wanted to run from the wrenching ordeal ahead. Yet he surrendered to God: "Not my will but yours be done" (Luke 22:42). He chose to drink the cup of suffering.

As the soldiers prepared to crucify him, they offered him a different cup, "wine mixed with myrrh" (Mark 15:23), a drink commonly given to those about to be crucified in order to dull the excruciating pain of hammering in the nails. The agony of Gethsemane, his arrest and trial, the flogging and the crown of thorns, falling under the impossible weight of the cross—he had already endured so much suffering, why not accept the drink and gain some slight relief now? The temptation to purchase oblivion through the drugged wine must have been great. As Klaas Schilder suggests:

> Never did the danger of a break between a whole series of the years of His life and this one moment of driven spikes and grinning faces threaten as overwhelmingly as it did now. . . . The life-work accomplished in thirty-three years is now in danger of drowning in a single cup of myrrh. But the human soul of Christ did not accentuate this moment at the cost of introducing discord into the logic of His whole life. The cup of myrrh did not interfere with the course of His obedience to God.[2]

When they offered him the drink, Jesus refused it (Mark 15:23). Instead, he drank his cup of suffering to the dregs, choosing to experience pain's full force. According to Frank Lake:

> The incarnate Word went into almost total silence, and into such darkness that He could not be seen by human eyes during those three hours in which He bore the dreadful limits of redemptive identification with all the worst forms of human suffering. . . . Neither the anxiety of commitment he experienced in Gethsemane, which made his sweat like drops of blood fall to the ground, nor the anxiety of separation in the final dereliction, diverted him for one moment from his path of obedient redemptive suffering.[3]

Despite extreme temptations along the way, he never departed from this path.

RUNNING FROM THE PAIN

Of course, the path Christ trod is not one we naturally choose. Charlie Brown's friend, Linus, in the comic strip *Peanuts*, illustrates the way we generally respond to suffering and problems. He tells Charlie Brown, "I don't like to face problems head on. I think the best way to solve problems is to avoid them. This is a distinct philosophy of mine. No problem is so big or so complicated that it can't be run away from." So Charlie Brown naively asks, "What if everyone was like you? What if everyone in the whole world suddenly decided to run away from his problems?" Linus retorts, "Well, at least we'd all be running in the same direction!"

Linus's problem-solving philosophy is by far the most popular. "Fearing the pain involved," Scott Peck observes, "almost all of us, to greater or lesser degree, attempt to avoid problems. . . . We attempt to skirt around problems rather than meet them head on. We attempt to get out of them rather than suffer through them." What happens as a result? Peck maintains that our determination to "avoid problems and the emotional suffering inherent in them" is the *primary* cause of mental illness. He quotes Carl Jung: "Neurosis is always a substitute for legitimate suffering."[4]

Our American culture, however, has difficulty allowing that suffering *is* legitimate. In 1963 Helmut Thielicke, a German preacher and theologian, visited the United States. Later, when asked by reporters what disturbed him most about America, he voiced concern that Americans did not know how to deal with suffering, nor did they expect suffering to be part of life. "Again and again," he said, "I have the feeling that suffering is regarded as something which is fundamentally inadmissible, disturbing, embarrassing and not to be endured."[5] Although Thielicke made that observation forty years ago, little has changed. It still is un-American to suffer, for it is out of keeping with our inalienable rights to life, liberty and the pursuit of happiness.

So we work hard to avoid suffering. As we saw in the last chapter, we often evade it by turning to various "behavioral narcotics" such as work, possessions, relationships, thrills, drugs and watching television. Even religion may become an escape route. A sexual abuse victim who became a Christian described how she avoided her pain: "I survived in 'Christian' ways—doing ministry for God, sharing my testimony, attending workshops and conferences, running to church meetings." Yet underneath she was still operating on the assumption that had governed her life as a non-Christian: "It's too scary to face your grief and sadness so run with all your might."[6]

In addition to escape mechanisms, we also develop response patterns to blunt pain and avoid facing it head-on. In *The Healing Path*, Dan Allender identifies four such approaches as paranoid, fatalistic, heroic and optimistic. Although we may use them all, one becomes our dominant way of responding. Allender summarizes them as follows:

The paranoiac avoids pain by seeing it everywhere and with

everyone. He avoids disappointment by never being surprised by sorrow. The fatalist avoids pain by accepting it as normal and part of the impersonal "luck" of life. The hero avoids pain by seizing it as an opportunity to grow without ever acknowledging need or weakness. The optimist avoids pain by seeing all the good surrounding it in other areas of life.[7]

FACING THE PAIN

The arms of Jesus on the cross—open, extended, reaching out— offer a radical alternative to our escape routes and pain avoidance mechanisms. They beckon us to embrace suffering, not evade it; to accept and actively bear anguish, not avoid it. Jesus became a "man of sorrows and acquainted with grief" (Isaiah 53:3 KJV). To walk the healing path, we too must be willing to engage the sorrow and grief in our own lives.

When pilots first attempted to break the sound barrier, the only way they could fly faster than the speed of sound was to direct their airplane into a straight dive. That made it extremely dangerous, for as they approached and passed through the sound barrier, the shock waves and sonic boom shook the plummeting aircraft and caused it to spin out of control. Consequently, the first couple of pilots who broke the sound barrier lost their lives. Their planes crashed because they couldn't pull them out of the dive.

Finally a pilot was able to complete the attempt. Unlike the earlier pilots, when the plane began to shake and spin as it approached and broke through the sound barrier, he didn't pull back on the stick to slow the plane down. Instead, he pushed the stick forward into the dive, accelerating even more. Surprisingly, the acceleration counteracted the effects of the shock waves and sonic boom on the plane. The shaking and spinning subsided, and he could bring the plane out of the dive.

The same is true for healing human hurts: The way to healing is to face the pain. Instead of pulling back, we push into the pain and then through it. Are we willing to do that in relation to our hurts? To embark on a journey into our dark places? To embrace our sorrows? To engage the suffering in our life?

In Hannah Hurnard's popular spiritual allegory *Hinds' Feet on High Places*, there is a point where God calls Much-Afraid to make Suffering and Sorrow companions on her journey. Knowing the treacherous path ahead, she can't understand why her faithful Shepherd would send her such unwanted, unattractive fellow travelers:

> "I can't go with them," she gasped. "I can't. I can't. O my Shepherd, why do you do this to me? How can I travel in their company? It is more than I can bear. You tell me that the mountain way itself is so steep and difficult that I cannot climb it alone. Then why, oh why, must you make Sorrow and Suffering my companions? Couldn't you have given Joy and Peace to go with me, to strengthen me, and encourage me and help me on this difficult way? I never thought you would do this to me.[8]

We may find ourselves reacting similarly when God appoints sorrow and suffering as sojourners on our pilgrimage to wholeness. We may argue with the Lord and plead for more pleasant traveling companions. But we will make little progress until we accept them as friends on our sacred healing journey.

STEPPING INTO THE PAIN

What is involved in embracing the pain? What might engaging suffering entail? Much depends on the nature and depth of the hurt. But the path to healing will likely involve several steps, including breaking through denial, recovering painful memories, owning anger, admitting our guilt, grieving losses and even descending into depression.

Breaking through denial. The truth will set you free—but first it may make you miserable. All of us have developed elaborate ways of staying in denial, of refusing to face the truth about our hurts. Often when people talk about some hurtful happening—for example, their parents' divorce—they trivialize their pain, saying:

- "It really wasn't that big of a deal."

- "We all have our share of suffering. Why should I be exempt?"

- "Given their backgrounds, they did the best they could. They shouldn't have stayed together just because of me."

- "They didn't really mean to hurt me."

- "It was partly my fault. I really made it hard on them when I was growing up. I really have no right to blame them."

- "You can't make excuses for yourself because of what your parents did. You just have to get on with your life."

- "What's past is past. There's no point dwelling on it."

Although a measure of truth inhabits these statements, they are often protective devices used to avoid the agony of the divorce. And by denying their hurt, they impede the process of healing.

Several years ago God used the words of a counselor to break through my denial about the pain bound up with my childhood years. From age seven to age twelve, I attended a missionary boarding school in India. Located in Kodaikanal, a scenic hill-station, the school served the children of North American Protestant missionaries who worked in south India. In addition to receiving an excellent education, I established deep friendships there. Committed Christian teachers, administrators and houseparents nurtured me and provided positive role models. But attending school at Kodai meant living five hundred miles away from my parents eight to nine months each year.

One day in talking to a counselor, I was accentuating the positive aspects of my boarding school experience, something I typically tended to do. His response caught me off guard. "All that may be true," he interjected, "but the fact is no seven-year-old is ready for such long periods of separation and emotional independence from his parents." His next words stunned me: *"It sure must have hurt!"*

Like a boxer dazed by an unexpected jab from his opponent, I staggered for a moment. Then I regained my balance and managed to change the subject. But the Holy Spirit kept reminding me of his words. *Did it really hurt?* I wondered. Had I buried the pain so deeply that I was unable to get in touch with it? I wanted to know. So I prayed and invited the Spirit to "guide me into all truth" and, if necessary, to allow any painful feelings to surface.

Over the next six months, God used a variety of things to answer my prayer. My heart had been wounded by my boarding school experience. It did hurt. Unpleasant memories and emotions—sadness, loneliness and anger—came bubbling up. My typical boarding school "litany of praise" was my way of keeping a lid on those hurtful feelings, a means of denial to protect myself from pain.

Facing truth can be agonizing. Before causing you to feel better, it may cause you to feel worse. But healing and honesty are bound up together. To bring our wounds to the cross, we have to look at them and acknowledge we are wounded. We cannot confess to God what we will not first admit to ourselves.

Recovering painful memories. Buried memories of particular hurtful experiences may begin to surface as we walk the healing path. Like putting together a jigsaw puzzle, sometimes we recover such memories gradually, piece by piece. At other times, they rush in and overwhelm us like flash flood waters.

A sexual abuse victim expressed to me how difficult recovering memories of abuse was for her: "No one wants to go back and look at that kind of pain. And it seemed like every new memory revealed

a higher degree of abuse. I had to go back and experience that violation over and over again, and to live with those events like they had
just happened yesterday, until I could learn to let them go." Time
and again she had found Jesus in the midst of her terror-filled memories. He gave her courage and strength to press into them. Compas-
sionately and sensitively, he ministered to the frightened, confused,
sad little child within. She always found him faithful. Yet she confessed, "Even after everything I know and have experienced about
what God does through this process, I still have to fight off major fear
just at the thought of facing new memories."

Memory recovery can occur in different ways. Sometimes, for example, God uses dreams and nightmares as wake-up calls for dealing
with terrifying trauma. Our conscious mind is unwilling to face past
hurts, so they emerge in the less threatening realm of the subcon-
scious while we are asleep. Repressed feelings such as anger, fear,
shame and grief often appear symbolically and indirectly in our
dreams. So the Spirit who intercedes for us and groans with us (Romans 8:26-27) uses them as contact points to guide us into truth.
Nonetheless, it's still disturbing to wake up in a cold sweat at three
a.m. during a nightmare.

Flashbacks are another common instrument of the Spirit. One
day when Ted Roberts[9] was a student at Asbury Seminary, he was
walking across campus after an eleven o'clock class. Suddenly the
shrill sound of the local fire station's noon siren pierced his ears. In
a moment, Ted was no longer in Wilmore, Kentucky; he was in Viet-
nam. The siren sounded exactly like the one he had heard there during enemy rocket attacks. But he wasn't merely remembering it; he
was reliving it. Instinctively he ran for cover, jumping into a dump-
ster next to a building. Embarrassed as he realized where he actually
was, he quickly crawled out of it and checked to see if anyone was
watching. His flashback, triggered by a familiar sound, uncovered
the unhealed trauma of his wartime experience.

Owning anger. Anger can be a frightening emotion, especially if we were raised in an environment where we were not allowed to feel or express it. To admit to anger would unleash the lava fires of our volcanic rage and surely result in destructive chaos. We would explode and fly out of control, so we work hard at repression and make sure the lid is sealed shut.

Several years ago I received a telephone call from Gena, a woman who had been in a church youth group I had worked with years earlier. Now she was in her mid-thirties, married with several children. Gena had been seeing a counselor and was beginning to recover buried memories of her father sexually abusing her at an early age. As she talked, I heard terror in her voice, for she didn't want to remember those awful things. But what frightened her most was her rage toward her father. She wanted to *murder* him.

All her life Gena had turned her ferocious anger on herself, even to the point of occasionally cutting and burning her own body. Although her way of expressing anger was self-destructive, it had become familiar and predictable. Now, as her repressed memories were surfacing, Gena was *feeling* anger toward her father for the first time, and it scared her to death. Like a blazing forest fire, she feared that her flaming rage would burn out of control and harm someone.

Mary, a woman in her forties, had also been sexually abused by her father. When she began seminary, her memories were buried so deeply that she had no conscious recollection of them. Then in her second semester, God began to draw back the curtain, and with the help of a skilled counselor, she began to remember. As the repressed memories of abuse came up, so did the anger. "There were times that semester," she told me later, "the anger was so intense I felt I was going to explode. So I would drive out to an open field in the country where I would shake my fist and scream at the top of my voice. I was angry at my father, at God, at the unfairness of it, at myself for the way I let it affect me. And I would shout until I was hoarse."

Anger can become a wild, violent, even dangerous emotion when it's been bottled up inside for years. For many, the healing path involves the fearful, unpleasant task of stepping directly into it.

Admitting our guilt. Another painful but necessary step toward healing involves admitting our guilt. All of us have not only been sinned against; we have sinned ourselves. Unjust suffering has been inflicted on us, but in our reactions we have turned to sinful attitudes and behaviors. As a result of wrongs done to us, we, in turn, have wrongfully hurt others and ourselves.

One day Melanie saw with devastating clarity the vow she made in response to her father's sexual abuse. She expressed it like this: "I'll 'murder' myself. I'll never let myself become the joyful, gifted, beautiful person I was created and destined to be." Instead of spreading her wings and flying like an eagle, she vowed to clip them so she could only hobble on the ground. This was her way of getting back at her father. Seeing her unable to fly would make him feel guilty for what he did. She was also getting back at God. By refusing to fly she was saying, "Because you didn't protect me, I won't become the person you created me to be."

When the angel of the Lord wrestled with Jacob (Genesis 32:22-32), he kept asking, "What is your name?" Finally Jacob admitted, "My name is Jacob—Deceiver, Heel-grabber." In the same way, as Melanie realized what she had done, the Lord questioned her about her name, and she finally confessed, "My name is Murderer." This was risky, for it meant she would no longer be able to blame her father or God. She would have to attempt flying. But like Jacob, when she admitted who she was, she was given a new name and transformed into a new person. Stifled spiritual gifts and graces burst forth. Soon she was airborne.

Acknowledging our guilt may also mean coming to terms with how our sinful reactions to hurts have hurt others, particularly in our own family. As he was in the process of recovery from addiction, Don

Crossland one day drove by the university his daughter had attended, causing images of her to flood his mind.

> I saw in my mind various images of her. Although she had many friends, in my mind I pictured her alone in her little car crying. The Holy Spirit was allowing me to experience some of the hurt my daughter had experienced because of my insensitivity. The Holy Spirit also reminded me that I had only visited her three times in four years and that I hadn't called her while she was there. I saw how negligent I have been because of my addiction. I was sobbing so deeply that I could hardly see to drive. Filled with sorrow and grief, I returned to my room and fell onto the bed. Throughout the night, I felt the hurt that I caused my family.[10]

Grieving losses. Whenever we are deprived of something we value, or something we need and expect, we experience loss. We grieve when we allow ourselves to feel sadness over our losses, and to grieve properly takes time; the deeper the loss, the longer the grief process.

Unfortunately, many of us have suffered losses for which we were not allowed to grieve. The wounds associated with these losses may be covered with scar tissue, but the infection of unresolved grief still festers within. Healing may require reopening those wounds to remove the infection and dealing with the unfinished business of grief.

Julie Woodley was in her late thirties when she finally grieved the losses she had experienced as an eighteen-year-old who ran away from home to escape from an abusive father. "For the first time in my life," she writes, "I felt the full force of that 18 year old girl's grief. Actually, God opened a floodgate of grief. I started replaying scenes from my childhood, scenes of abandonment and rejection. There was a deep well of sadness in my heart. After years of running from it, I had finally tapped into it, allowing myself to feel it and pour out of me."[11]

We have to grieve not only over the pain of things that were but also over things that were not. Because of hurts we experienced, possibilities were lost. One person expressed it to me like this: "As I could see more clearly what kind of damage my childhood had done to me, I had to grieve for all the things I couldn't be when I was little, as well as for the pain it cost me later on. Trust and security, carefree play time, the sense of being cherished and loved—I had to grieve those losses. I had to grieve the years of messed-up relationship with God, years I knew I could never have back. I had to grieve over who I had become and what I had done along the way, and I had to grieve the loss of all my hiding places."

Jesus said, "Blessed are those who mourn, for they will be comforted" (Matthew 5:4). But he never said mourning would be pleasant, especially the kind that may be necessary for healing deep pain and loss.

Descending into depression. As feelings of hurt and anger, sadness and grief come to the surface, they may thrust us into the darkness of depression. Again Julie Woodley describes how this happened to her:

> For a year I fell into a deep depression. Obviously, this wasn't my idea of healing. At the time, I felt like I was moving "backwards" instead of "forwards." I couldn't speak except to pray. In three months, I lost fifty pounds, shrinking from a size 10 to a size 3. In a strange way, even though I knew the hope of Christ, my heart felt bereft of hope. The sadness and grief kept pouring out of me and there was no end in sight.[12]

Those who find themselves in such thick darkness will often need to see a physician or psychiatrist who can prescribe anti-depressant medication. In some cases, they may even need to be hospitalized. Above all, they will need a supportive network—family members and friends, a small group within the church, a pastor or counselor—who will guide, encourage and, most of all, love them through the dark tunnel of pain.

Like the paralyzed man who was brought to Jesus (Mark 2:1-12), we may be emotionally paralyzed by depression. The bedridden man couldn't bring himself to Jesus but had to be brought by his friends who lowered him down through the roof. And when Jesus saw their faith—not the paralytic's, for it was immobilized too—he spoke the forgiving word and commanded the man to rise and walk. So, too, those in the grip of depression and unable to move need others to carry them in prayer to Jesus and believe for them.

STANDING IN YOUR PAIN AT THE CROSS

Jesus' open arms on the cross call us to open our arms, to embrace suffering in order to find healing for our hurts. But in light of what it might entail—breaking out of denial, recovering painful memories, owning anger, admitting guilt, grieving losses, even descending into depression—how can we do it? In Paul's words, "Who is sufficient for these things?" (2 Corinthians 2:16). Even if initially we can *embrace* the pain, how will we ever *endure* it?

The answer lies at the foot of the cross. Standing there, we are given the strength. As we gaze at his open arms, as we look to him for help, Christ's courage and fortitude becomes ours. His cross not only provides the pattern of actively bearing suffering; it also offers the power we need to confront the darkness in our souls. We discover that Jesus' open arms are also God's everlasting arms, embracing us and bearing us up. No matter how deep, no dreadful abyss is ever bottomless. Always, always "underneath are the everlasting arms" (Deuteronomy 33:27 NIV).

As we abide in him, so Christ, the one who opened himself to unimaginable dread and despair, abides in us. His courage and determination is imparted to us. As we stand beneath the cross like a patient facing a painful operation, we are able to say to Jesus, our great physician and surgeon, "I am ready." In Christ, we can open our arms to embrace the pain and endure the suffering necessary for healing.

Christ's grace not only enables us to embrace and endure suffering, it also transforms us through our suffering. Suffering we feared would be destructive becomes redemptive. Self-destroying, spirit-depleting suffering turns into self-enlarging, spirit-strengthening suffering. The suffering we were so determined to avoid increases our passion for life. We discover treasures in the darkness (Isaiah 45:3).

Jacob was exhausted after wrestling all night with the angel (Genesis 32:22-32). His hip was out of joint, and for the rest of his life, he walked with a limp. But he named the place Peniel (the face of God) because there he experienced a profound encounter with God. As we walk into the anguish, as we wrestle with truth that wounds, we too may walk away exhausted and limping. But like Jacob, whose name was changed that day to Israel, we will go away transformed and grateful, knowing we have seen the face of Jesus, our crucified Lord.

QUESTIONS FOR PERSONAL OR GROUP REFLECTION

1. What has generally been your response to pain? Have there been instances in your life when you have courageously walked into and through pain? What has happened at other times when you may have tried to walk away from or around pain?

2. Scott Peck maintains that our determination to avoid problems and the emotional suffering inherent in them is the primary cause of mental illness. Do you agree with him? If not, what do you believe the consequences are of trying to avoid problems and their accompanying emotional pain?

3. In the allegory *Hinds' Feet on High Places*, the main character's God-appointed traveling companions are aptly named Sorrow

and Suffering. To her surprise, at the end of the journey they reveal that they have been Peace and Joy in disguise all along. Have you ever found that sorrow and suffering were a pathway to peace and joy? Do you believe that God has this as an ultimate purpose?

4. Have you ever persisted in prayer for someone in the grip of depression and been a part of the supportive network that loved that person through the dark tunnel of pain? Has someone done the same for you? Faithful friends can hold up our arms to embrace the pain, but only Christ can give us the strength to endure it. Have you found this to be true?

8

Father, Forgive Them

> *The Cross of Jesus not only teaches us to forgive others, even in extremis, but it inspires and enables us to do so. Nothing else will.*

DOUGLAS WEBSTER

For years, Katherine Birge burned with resentment toward her father. Although he was a loved and respected pastor, he unleashed a vicious, uncontrollable temper at home. As a young girl Katherine repeatedly felt the brunt of it. Having been hurt by him, she wanted to hurt him in return. Even after he died, she says, "I carried within myself a heavy burden of hatred almost as though I were entitled to it. I believed that injustice had been done to me and that I had the right to resent that injustice."[1]

Finally, as a woman in her forties, she was able to forgive her father. Her breakthrough came on December 13, 1970. The night before, she had gone to bed with two different thoughts in her head. One revolved around her hatred toward her father, the other around a question a little girl had asked that day in her second-grade class: "How come Jesus got to be so great when we're just nothing?"

Katherine had assured the little girl, "We're *not* nothing. We are sons and daughters of God." The girl seemed pleased by her answer. Still, Katherine kept pondering her question, especially the part about Jesus being so great. So she dozed off both resenting her father and wondering about Jesus. Katherine then describes what happened the next day:

> I woke up early the next morning. I heard no voice and I saw no vision, but I experienced the impression of Christ on the cross saying the words, "Father, forgive them. They know not what they do." At that moment it was as though a tremendous weight was lifted from me. My resentment was a heavy load that I had been carrying, and suddenly I was freed from it! I was free not through any virtue of my own but through the grace of God. Early in the morning, in the half light between darkness and dawn, on December 13, 1970, a miracle happened to me. I was free! My hatred for my father was not only a painful load for me to carry; it had blocked my relationship with God. It had poisoned my life! And suddenly I was free!
>
> That morning was rich with spiritual blessings. It was a mystic moment when I felt as though time had the texture of eternity and as though heaven's rays shone all around me. If Jesus could accept crucifixion in the spirit of forgiveness, then surely I should be able to forgive my father for any "wrong" he might have done to me.[2]

For Katherine, the words Jesus uttered from the cross—"Father, forgive them; for they do not know what they are doing" (Luke 23:34)—provided a pattern for forgiving her father and released in her the power to forgive him. As a result, she was delivered from her bondage to bitterness and set free to love her father. She also understood as never before the answer to the little girl's question "How come Jesus got to be so great?"

Throughout his ministry Jesus consistently stressed that as God has forgiven us, we in turn ought to forgive others. In the Lord's Prayer, he taught us to say:

Forgive us our debts,
    as we also have forgiven our debtors. (Matthew 6:12)

On another occasion he commanded his disciples, "Whenever you stand praying, forgive, if you have anything against anyone" (Mark 11:25). When Peter inquired how many times he was obligated to forgive, Jesus insisted, "Not seven times, but, I tell you, seventy-seven times" (Matthew 18:22). He then told a story about an unforgiving servant (Matthew 18:23-34). Although his master had forgiven his immense debt, the servant refused to forgive a minor amount owed to him by a fellow servant. When the master found out what the servant had done, he had the servant thrown in jail. Jesus warned his disciples, "So my heavenly Father will also do to every one of you, if you do not forgive your brother or sister from your heart" (Matthew 18:35).

Jesus not only consistently preached radically extending forgiveness to others, he also practiced it. And he practiced it when it was incomprehensibly difficult—as he was hanging on a cross. The victim of gross injustice, his body wracked with pain, the vicious taunts of his enemies ringing in his ears, he gathered his strength and cried out, "Father, forgive them. They don't know what they are doing."

The Christian imperative to forgive those who have inflicted pain on us is a call to imitate Jesus. However, we are not called to imitate Christ in our own strength. Like Katherine Birge, we discover that as we will to forgive, he imparts his strength to us. The word of forgiveness spoken *on* the cross is also spoken *in* us.

THE SEVEN STEPS OF FORGIVENESS

I cannot overemphasize the importance of forgiveness in the healing of human hurts. Forgiveness unlocks the door to healing, restoration, freedom and renewal. Until we open that door, we will remain stuck in the past, destined to carry the hurt and burden forever without hope of a restored heart or a renewed future. Charles

Kraft is right: "There is no greater blockage to a person's receiving healing from God than that person's refusal to forgive others."[3] We will never find healing for our hurts until, like Jesus, we say, "Father, forgive them."

What then does true forgiveness—Jesus called it forgiving "from the heart" (Matthew 18:35)—involve? There are actually seven steps or elements in true forgiveness. Steps 1-3 are directed toward the past and are the indispensable preparation if forgiving from the heart is to take place. Steps 4-5 focus on the present and are really the core or essence of forgiveness. Steps 6-7 are oriented toward the future and the possibility of starting over, which forgiveness creates.

Let's examine these steps one at a time.

Preparing to forgive.

1. *Facing the facts.* Forgiveness begins when we are ruthlessly honest about what was done to us. We don't cover up what happened, explain it away, blame ourselves or make excuses for the other person. Squarely and realistically, we face the truth: "I was violated and sinned against. I was hurt. What they did was wrong." As C. S. Lewis says, "Real forgiveness means looking steadily at the sin, the sin that is left over without any excuse, after all allowances have been made, and seeing it in all its horror, dirt, meanness and malice, and nevertheless being wholly reconciled to the person who has done it."[4]

In facing facts, it is important to be specific. General acknowledgments of wrong followed by sweeping generalizations of forgiveness won't do. For example, when a woman admitted to me, "My mother did some mean things to me when I was growing up," I probed with a question: "Can you describe a particular incident when she hurt you?"

Tearfully she responded, "One Friday night when I was in high school, my boyfriend had come over to our house to pick me up for a date. As I walked down the stairs to meet him, right in front of him my mother said to me, 'Why did you wear *that* dress? You look *awful* in it!' I can't tell you how humiliated I was by what she said."

After telling her how sorry I was, I said, "Are you willing to forgive your mother for what she said to you that night?"

For many, the first step in forgiving will involve what we spoke about in the last chapter—getting out of denial. Truth can be hard to bear, and at times, we will go to great lengths to avoid it.

In 1997 I was conducting a seminar on forgiveness in the Baltic nation of Estonia. Katrina, a woman who attended, compared her own denial to the recent behavior of her alcoholic father. A week before the seminar, she and her husband had visited her father at his summer home. When they arrived, he was drunk and lying around with his shirt off. They noticed a place on his back that was badly scratched and swollen. When they looked closely, they found a large nail embedded in it.

"You've got to go to the hospital immediately," they told him. "There's a nail in your back that needs to be removed. Otherwise, it's going to get infected."

But her drunken father wouldn't listen. "I'm fine," he insisted, "It doesn't hurt that much. There's no nail there. You're just wasting my time."

After arguing with him for awhile, they finally forced him to get in the car and took him to the hospital against his will. Only when the doctor showed him the nail he had pulled from his back did Katrina's father believe it had been there.

"When I came to this seminar, I was like my father," Katrina admitted. "There were nails in my soul which were causing pain. But I had gotten so used to them, I hardly felt them. My heart was pricked all over with the nails of my hurts. They were old and rusty, big and small nails, but like my stubborn father I didn't want to admit they were there or that it hurt. I am thankful that during our sessions, God showed me the nails. Before I could forgive those who drove them in, I had to admit they were there."

Like Katrina, we may carry nails in our hearts hammered in by the actions of others. Forgiveness begins by acknowledging they are there and looking at them intently.

2. *Feeling the hurt.* In the 1960's TV series *Dragnet*, detective Joe Friday would often say as he was conducting investigations, "Just the facts, ma'am, just the facts."

Forgiveness begins with facing the facts but then goes further. More than "just the facts," we must connect with the feelings bound up with the facts—feelings like rejection, loneliness, fear, anger, shame and depression that still reverberate in us today. Sometimes a person can recount horrendous things done to them without blinking an eye. They are so matter-of-fact about the details that you wonder if they are related to Mr. Spock, the extremely rational, devoid-of-affect character on the original *Star Trek* TV series. Their emotions are so painful and threatening they have simply disconnected from them. And so we have to persistently ask, "What were you *feeling* when that happened to you?"

Answering that question can be extremely difficult. No one wants to reexperience such unpleasant feelings. Better then to deny them, it seems, or sweep them under the rug. But we can't reach the threshold of forgiveness until we recover, at least in some measure, the feelings bound up with the painful facts. Henri Nouwen says:

> The great challenge is *living* your wounds through instead of *thinking* them through. It is better to cry than to worry, better to feel your wounds deeply than to understand them, better to let them enter into your silence than to talk about them. The choice you face constantly is whether you are taking your wounds to your head or to your heart. In your head you can analyze them, find their causes and consequences, and coin words to speak and write about them. But no final healing is

likely to come from that source. You need to let your wounds go down into your heart.[5]

3. *Confronting our hate.* Forgiving involves letting go of hatred or resentment toward the persons who have wounded us. But again, before we can let go of something we have to acknowledge it's there. We must admit we resent those who wronged us, for a part of us hates them for what they did.

Carol, the wife of a thirty-five-year-old seminary student, had been depressed for over a month. Three members of her Sunday school class (myself included) were counseling and praying with her, hoping to discern the cause for the dark cloud hanging over her. When we asked if she had ever been depressed before, Carol began to talk about her husband Martin's adulterous affair five years earlier. She had been depressed then, but she assured us good had come out of it. God had used his shameful sin to wake him up and to bring him to Christ. Several years later he felt called to pastoral ministry.

Sensing her reluctance to face her anger over what he had done, I said, "You must have been furious at Martin when you learned about his affair."

"Yes, I was," she answered. "But I am sure he wouldn't have had the affair if I'd have been a better wife."

"I'm sure you could have been a better wife," I responded, "but your failures didn't give him a right to commit adultery. The truth is Martin was a jerk. You must have wanted to rip his eyes out!"

By speaking so forcefully, I was trying to give Carol permission to own her anger and resentment toward Martin, but to no avail. For the next forty-five minutes, every time we encouraged her to do that, she would invariably blame herself. Although what he did was wrong, she kept insisting the affair was her fault more than his.

I understood now why she was depressed. She had a legitimate reason to be angry with Martin. He had violated their marriage covenant, betrayed her trust and sinned against her. But instead of owning her anger, she preferred to turn it on herself.

Forgiveness is *not* blaming ourselves for what happened. We may not be completely innocent, but what our victimizers did was unjustifiable. They are to blame for our pain, and there is a part of us that hates them for it. Forgiveness requires the courage to confront our hatred.

In the first three steps of forgiveness we own what happened in the past and how we feel about it. We face the wrongs, feel the hurt and admit our hate. Now we stand at a crossroad. We have a present decision to make: to forgive or not to forgive. The next two steps are truly the heart of forgiveness.

The heart of forgiveness.
4. *Bearing the pain.* When others have wronged us, there is a demanding voice within us that cries out, "What they did isn't right. They ought to *pay* for what they've done." This is a God-given voice. The desire to see justice in our own—and all—relationships has been planted in our hearts by God.

So when we forgive, do we ignore the divinely implanted desire for justice and set it aside? No. The sin, the injustice, must be taken seriously. But instead of achieving justice by insisting the guilty party pay for the wrong, we choose to pay ourselves. Though innocent, we choose to bear the pain of the injustice. In forgiveness, as the Scripture says, "mercy triumphs over judgment" (James 2:13). It triumphs, however, not by ignoring judgment but by bearing it.

In the Old Testament, several different words in the original Hebrew are rendered "forgive" in our English Bible versions. One of the words is the Hebrew verb *nasa*, which in more than a dozen places is translated "to forgive." In over 150 places, however, *nasa* is rendered "to carry" or "to bear." Old Testament writers understood the close connection between forgiving and bearing. Whenever we forgive, we bear pain.

That's why forgiveness is always costly. Parents, for example, may choose to forgive a wayward child. But what that child has done broke their hearts and brought shame on the family. Instead of demanding the child suffer for causing them to suffer, forgiveness will entail the parents' vicarious suffering, their sacrificial bearing of the pain inflicted on them. Theologian H. R. Macintosh says: "In every great forgiveness there is enshrined a great agony."[6]

Of course, the ultimate example of the costliness of forgiveness is the cross of Christ. The Scripture says, "He himself bore our sins in his body on the cross" (1 Peter 2:24). He took on himself the guilt, punishment and shame of our sins. We deserved to suffer for them but instead, God in Christ carried them in his own being. God did not overlook our sins or pretend they didn't matter but bore the pain and the judgment himself. Christ, the Judge, allowed himself to be judged in our place. To a much lesser degree, whenever we forgive others, we do the same thing: we take the punishment they deserve, absorbing it ourselves. We bear the pain.

5. *Releasing those who have wronged us.* Although forgiveness does not set aside the demands of justice, it still seems to run crossgrain to our natural sense of fair play. "Wait a minute!" we protest, "this isn't fair. You want me to forgive them. But if I do, they're going to walk away scot-free. And they're the ones who are at fault here—not me. They ought to pay for what they've done."

In part, our anger and resentment is our way of regaining control of an unfair situation and getting back at the persons who have wronged us. It's our attempt to even the score. After all, don't they deserve that?

But forgiving means releasing our offenders and turning them over to God. It's saying, "I know what they've done and I feel the pain of it, but I choose *not* to be the one who determines what is justice for them." When we forgive we relinquish the roles of judge, jury and executioner and turn them over to God.

The New Testament conveys this idea by the Greek verb *aphiemi*, one of the words most commonly rendered "to forgive" in our English Bible versions. In most instances, however, *aphiemi* is translated "to leave" or "to let go," and involves voluntarily releasing a person or thing over which one has legal or actual control.

When we forgive, then, we relinquish control of the persons who have wronged us. We quit playing God in their lives. No longer will we determine what is just for them or make sure they get what they deserve. Thus, forgiveness is an act of faith. We turn the ones who have wronged us over to God. We *entrust* them to God, saying, "Vengeance is not mine, but Thine alone." And like all faith acts, forgiveness contains an element of risk. What if God doesn't get even with those who have wronged us? What if God chooses to extend mercy to them?

A young man who had suffered greatly as a result of his parents' selfishness and eventual divorce expressed the risk involved in forgiving his parents: "When it came to forgiving my parents, I had to choose to put down the sword I thought I had a right to. But when I put down my sword, it was like I put down myself." His resentment and his role as sword-wielding executioner had become a part of his identity. What of himself would remain if he gave them up?

David Augsburger notes that the word *forgive* in the English language is "an extended, expanded, strengthened form of the verb *to give*. By intensifying the verb we speak of giving at its deepest level, of self-giving, of *giving forth* and *giving up* deeply held parts of the self."[7] By giving the people who have wronged us over to God, we also give ourselves to God. Parts of ourselves we have been holding are now entrusted to him. No wonder there is such healing power in forgiveness. When we release others and ourselves to God, we give up control, and then his presence and power are released in us.

Bearing the pain and releasing those who have wronged us constitute the heart of forgiveness. But I want to emphasize that forgiveness doesn't ignore or set aside the demands of justice. One might conclude that when we forgive, we refrain from any effort to hold those who have wronged us accountable for their behavior, leaving that totally up to God and to others. However, that simply is not true.

In the case of a sexual abuse victim, for example, forgiving the abuser is not incompatible with exposing or pressing legal charges against him or her. Forgiveness doesn't mean tolerating injustice. "Unfruitful works of darkness" should be exposed (Ephesians 5:11). Actions have consequences that evildoers must be forced to accept. When crimes have been committed, offenders should be turned over to the judicial system.

Bearing the pain and releasing those who have wronged us have to do with our *attitudes* toward those who have wronged us; seeking justice has to do with our *actions* toward them. These attitudes and actions are not opposed to each other. In fact, practicing forgiveness and promoting justice go hand in hand. Having made a decision to forgive, our concern in promoting justice is not to avenge ourselves or destroy our offenders but to protect ourselves and others in the community from future injury at the offender's hands. Furthermore, by insisting that offenders be held accountable for their actions, we are actually extending grace to them by offering them an opportunity to face the truth about themselves, admit their wrongdoing and turn from their wicked ways.

The last two steps in forgiveness aim toward the future and center around the possibility of new relationships—with ourselves and the persons who have wronged us.

Starting over.
6. *Assuming responsibility for ourselves.* As long as we blame others for our problems, we don't have to take responsibility for ourselves; they're on the hook. By releasing them, however, we let them off the hook. And where does that leave us? Now we're on the hook. We must

take responsibility and can no longer make excuses for ourselves.

Often people hesitate when challenged to forgive because in-stinctively they know that if they do, they will have no one to blame for their predicament. When confronted with his obesity, one man reacted defensively, "You'd be overweight too if you had a neurotic father like mine." What will happen if he forgives his father? He will have no excuse for his weight problem and no one to blame but himself.

Unfortunately, we live in a culture of victimization that encour-ages us to play the blame game. For many Americans, portraying one-self as a victim has even become an attractive pastime. A *Calvin and Hobbes* cartoon strip makes this point. In the first frame, as he trudges through the snow, Calvin declares to his tiger friend, Hobbes, "Noth-ing I do is my fault." In the next frame, the little boy stops to explain, "My family is dysfunctional and my parents won't empower me! Consequently, I'm not self-actualized!" In the third frame, Calvin pi-ously continues, "My behavior is addictive, functioning in a diseased process of toxic codependency! I need holistic healing and wellness before I'll accept any responsibility for my actions!" In the last frame, he stomps off triumphantly declaring, "I love the culture of victim-hood." To which the frustrated Hobbes finally exclaims, "One of us needs to stick his head in a bucket of ice water."

Forgiveness strikes a blow at the root of one's victim status. We may have been a victim, but we're not stuck there. By taking respon-sibility for ourselves, we declare that what happened doesn't define who we are. We have an identity apart from our pain.

That can be risky and frightening, of course. We may have grown to depend on our excuses and become comfortable with our victim identity. Losing an enemy whom we can resent and blame may dis-turb us more than losing a friend. We may be meeting needs by our holding on to our pain and resentment.

Yet how liberating it is when, by forgiving, we do accept responsibility for ourselves. The persons who have hurt us no longer exercise control over our lives. When we forgive we not only release them, we also release ourselves from them and set ourselves free to determine our destiny apart from our wounds.

7. *Longing for reconciliation.* The ultimate goal and purpose of forgiveness is reconciliation, or the restoration and renewal of broken relationships. Thus, forgiveness is not only about letting go of bitterness and revoking revenge. As healing and liberating as that is, it forms only the negative side of forgiveness. The positive side is reconciliation, the coming together of persons who have been alienated from each other.

According to some therapists, we should forgive an offender purely on the basis of self-interest. "Forgive," they tell us, "so you will feel better, get unstuck from your unfair past and stop allowing your offender to exert control over your life. Do this for *yourself*." And it's true. Forgiving others *is* in our best interest.

But from a Christian perspective, forgiving simply so I can get my hurts healed and get on with my life doesn't go far enough. It encompasses the negative purpose of forgiveness but fails to include the positive—reconciliation with the person who has offended me.

Of course, the *nature* and *extent* of reconciliation depend on a number of factors, the most important of which is the offender's willingness to be reconciled with us and to take the costly action necessary for its accomplishment. In many instances we won't be able to achieve the measure of reconciliation we desire. What do we do, for instance, when the offender refuses to be reconciled with us or persists in offensive behavior? On occasion we will have to settle for less than the best. On a reconciliation scale of one to ten, we may have to live with a three.

Still, forgiveness ought to put within us a longing for reconciliation. At first we may grudgingly say, "I'll forgive them, but I don't want to have anything to do with them ever again." And that may be a sufficient place to start. But as forgiveness does its work, it will change our attitude. We will begin to see our offenders through eyes of compassion. One day we will even find ourselves wishing good for them. Our longing for a reconciled relationship may so intensify that we grieve when it fails to work out.

FORGIVING AT THE CROSS

The process of forgiving someone who has wronged us brings us once again to the cross of Christ. In writing about someone who had inflicted pain on the Corinthian church, Paul makes this fascinating statement: "Anyone whom you forgive, I also forgive. What I have forgiven, if I have forgiven anything, has been for your sake in the presence of Christ" (2 Corinthians 2:10). Notice his last phrase, "in the presence of Christ."

Sometimes counselors place an empty chair across from a client and ask them to pretend the person who has wounded them is sitting in it. They are then encouraged to speak words of forgiveness to that person as if he or she were actually there. In some cases, it proves to be an effective technique in facilitating forgiveness.

As Christians, however, we should forgive not only in the presence of an offender but, following Paul's example, in the presence of Christ. And if a chair can help convey the presence of another person, what better way to convey Christ's presence than by imagining ourselves at the foot of the cross. There we bring our hurts; there we own our resentment and desire for revenge. And above all, there we receive strength to forgive.

As we stand at the cross, we must remember that initially forgiveness is more about a decision than an emotion. First and foremost, it is a matter of the will. We come to a place where we choose to forgive. We might be struggling with negative feelings toward those who have hurt us, and we may continue to do so for a considerable time. What is most important at first is our willingness. In forgiving, you send your will ahead by express; your emotions generally come later by slow freight.

But what if we are unwilling to forgive? The hurt is so great, the anger and resentment so intense that nothing within us wants to let go of it. Then we should pray, "Lord, make me willing to be made willing." As a Puritan preacher once advised, "If you can't come to God *with* a broken heart, come to God *for* one." So if you can't come to the cross *with* a willing heart to forgive, come there *for* one.

Several years ago, I had an intriguing thought. On the cross, if Jesus bore both the wrongs done to *him* and the wrongs done to *us*, then when he cried, "Father, forgive them," could it be he was offering forgiveness not only to those who had wronged him but also to those who have wronged us? If that is true, then in effect, Jesus has already extended forgiveness to the persons for what they did to us. So if we can't will to forgive them, we can pray, "Jesus, you live in me. Therefore speak the words in me and through me. Help me to join you in saying, 'Father, forgive them.' Even though I can't speak them myself, I can at least allow you to speak them in me."

Leanne Payne tells how Christ spoke the word of forgiveness in her one day as she struggled to let go of her hatred for an unforgivable thing someone had done to her:

> From this person I had suffered assaults that were irrational and weighted by envy, lying, and slander. But on this day a final act came to light, one that to me was and still is unthinkable, one designed to destroy me and all I held dear. The act went right to the core of me. In pain and amazement, I knew for the first time how in the passion of hate one person could kill another human being. . . .
>
> I fell to my knees and cried out to God for help. "Please do not let me hate," I cried over and over. Getting no relief, I phoned a friend to come over and help me pray. All afternoon, having

thrown myself face down over the living room ottoman, I cried out to God and my prayer partner cried out with me. . . . Then came a moment when instantly my pleading was interrupted by an amazing awareness of Christ in me, and from that center where He and I were mysteriously one, forgiveness was extended to my enemy. It was as if Christ in and through me forgave the person (who can explain such a thing?)—yet I too forgave.[8]

Like Leanne, we obtain grace in his presence to release resentment and revenge. As we wait at the cross, Jesus will speak the forgiving word in us.

The healing of our hurts and the transformation of our feelings toward those who have wounded us can then really begin. But often this part of the forgiveness process happens slowly—layer by layer. Sometimes after making the decision to forgive, our negative feelings toward the person actually intensify. Like taking the lid off a garbage can, our decision to forgive may release noxious odors that have been sealed up. Repressed emotions surface. Anger may burn more hotly than ever. Or we find ourselves overwhelmed with sadness. Choosing to forgive may cause the pain to intensify. Now that the lid is off, we begin remembering hurtful incidents. Agonizing pictures flood our minds. Old wounds open up all over again. We seem to be going backward, getting worse rather than better.

At this point we may be tempted to think, *I haven't really forgiven so-and-so. If I had, I wouldn't be experiencing such intense pain and resentment.* The truth is, forgiveness is both a crisis (a definite decision) and a process (releasing hurt and resentment and receiving healing at ever-deepening levels). We have made the decision to forgive, but we are still engaged in the process where many emotional twists and turns lurk along the way. So we don't need to start over. We simply need to reaffirm our will to forgive, asking the Lord to deepen it. We must also continue to offer our hurtful and hateful

feelings to God, praying, "Lord, heal the hurt and cleanse the hate."
As we do, we discover that God who has begun this good work in us,
is faithful to complete it (Philippians 1:6).

But the healing and cleansing of our hearts is not a one-shot deal.
In the crisis of a moment we can will to forgive, but working through
our hurt and bitterness happens slowly. We may even find Jesus'
charge to forgive "not seven times, but, . . . seventy-seven times"
(Matthew 18:22) applying to the same offense. At the cross, however,
grace awaits to see it through, to finish the good work of forgiveness
begun in us.

Do you need grace to begin the process of forgiving someone who
has wronged and wounded you? Do you need grace to continue as
you struggle with feelings of hurt and bitterness? Come to Calvary.
It is the place to forgive. Hear Jesus say, "Father, forgive them." God's
grace—initiating, sustaining, healing, transforming—is sufficient
and abundant there. It is grace to forgive.

QUESTIONS FOR PERSONAL OR GROUP REFLECTION

1. Have you ever forgiven someone who has hurt you deeply? What
   stands out in your memory of that experience?

2. Have you ever been caught up in "faulty forgiveness"? Covering
   up? Explaining away? Excusing the pain that others caused?
   Blaming yourself for the pain?

3. Is there someone you are in the process of forgiving now? Based
   on the seven steps outlined in the chapter, what step(s) are you engaged in now?

4. Personalize the following prayer: "Jesus, show me the truth about
   the nails in my soul. Remove them by your grace. Help me to feel
   the feelings as you reveal the facts. Give me the grace to admit the
   resentments I hold. Strengthen me to bear the pain that was di-

rected against me. Move in my heart that I would release to you those who have sinned against me, trusting you completely as the only righteous Judge. Instill responsibility in me. Show me how to get 'unstuck' and to reclaim my identity apart from my pain. May my heart beat with a longing for reconciliation as it accords with your will. Cause me to walk in forgiveness, Lord."

9

Love Your Enemies

*How then does love conquer? By asking not how the enemy treats
her but only how Jesus treated her. The love for our enemies
takes us along the way of the cross and into fellowship with
the Crucified. The more we are driven along this road, the more
certain is the victory of love over the enemy's hatred. For then
it is not the disciple's own love, but the love of Jesus Christ alone,
who for the sake of his enemies went to the cross and prayed
for them as he hung there.*

DIETRICH BONHOEFFER

In 1915, during a religious and ethnic conflict in which over a million Armenians were slaughtered by the Turks, a military unit attacked a village, murdering all the adults and taking the young women as hostages. In one home, after killing the parents, the officer in charge gave the daughters to the men in his command but kept the beautiful oldest daughter for himself. After several months of slavery and sexual abuse, she escaped from him and began to rebuild her life. Eventually she attended training school and became a nurse.

One night several years later, while she was working in a hospital intensive care unit, she recognized the face of a desperately ill patient. He was the officer who had enslaved and abused her and had murdered her parents. His comatose condition required round-the-clock attention and care. Only after a lengthy and difficult time during which he was mostly semiconscious did he begin to recover.

One day, as he was finally regaining his health, a doctor spoke to him about the nurse who had been caring for him. "What a fortunate man you are," he commented. "Without her constant devotion you would have never made it."

Later when they were alone, the officer stared at the nurse. "I've wanted for days to ask you, we've met before, haven't we?"

"Yes," the nurse nodded. "We've met before."

"I don't understand," he continued. "Why didn't you kill me when you had the opportunity? Why didn't you just let me die?"

"Because I am a follower of one who said, 'love your enemies,' " the nurse replied.[1]

Jesus' followers had been taught to love their neighbors and hate their enemies, but in his Sermon on the Mount, Jesus commanded them to love their enemies and pray for their persecutors (Matthew 5:43-44). He said to them, "I say to you that listen, Love your enemies, do good to those who hate you, bless those who curse you, pray for those who abuse you" (Luke 6:27-28). It is not enough to just forgive our enemies; Jesus calls us to love them as well.

By "enemies," I particularly have in mind those who have inflicted emotional pain and injury on us. We may never have viewed them as enemies before. In most cases they have been parents, siblings, spouses or close friends—those who ought to love us most yet by their hurtful words and actions have treated us as if we were enemies. In many cases, their "friendly fire" was far deadlier than any enemy fire, so the command to love our enemies is particularly appropriate to them.

As in the case of forgiving people, Jesus practiced what he preached about loving one's enemies, and he practiced it when it was most difficult: as he hung on the cross. Through his example we are able to determine what loving those who have treated us like enemies might mean for us. Two passages of Scripture, 1 Peter 2:18-25 and Romans 12:14-21, are particularly helpful in teaching us how to love our enemies. The first describes how Jesus showed love for his enemies as he hung on the cross; the second, what it means for us to love our enemies.

WHEN HE WAS ABUSED

Writing to fledgling Christian congregations who were experiencing increasing hostility and persecution, Peter reminds his readers how Christ responded when he was subjected to the unjust suffering of the cross. In 1 Peter 2:18-25, he speaks directly to Christian slaves who were being harshly mistreated. Some had been mercilessly beaten (Gk. *kolaphizein*, "to strike with the fist") by irate masters (1 Peter 2:20), an experience that Christ shared as he was beaten during the final hours of his life (Gk. *kolaphizein*; Matthew 26:67; Mark 14:65). And Christ, in his crucifixion, was also executed in the same manner as slaves.

Peter tells Christian slaves that Christ left them a fitting example by the way he endured unjust suffering, "so that you should follow in his steps" (1 Peter 2:21). He didn't suffer for any wrongdoing. Like the suffering servant of whom Isaiah had spoken centuries before,

> He committed no sin,
>   and no deceit was found in his mouth.
> (1 Peter 2:22; cf. Isaiah 53:9)

Jesus suffered for doing right. And how did he respond? Peter describes the pattern of patient endurance Jesus displayed.

"When he was abused, he did not return abuse" (1 Peter 2:23). Throughout the entire Passion ordeal, from the time he was brought before the high priest to the moment of his death, Jesus was subject to intense verbal abuse. Earlier we considered the mocking he endured. It began at his trial when the religious leaders and the guards

taunted and "kept heaping many other insults on him" (Luke 22:65). When he was turned over to Herod and his soldiers, they too "treated him with contempt and mocked him" (Luke 23:11). Later Pilate's soldiers jeered and made fun of him (Matthew 27:29-30). As he hung on the cross, those who passed by "derided him" and shook their heads (Mark 15:29). The chief priests and the scribes who stood there "were also mocking him among themselves" (Mark 15:31). Even the thieves who were crucified with him "taunted him" (Mark 15:32). In the final hours of his life, intense, unrelenting verbal abuse came at him from every direction. Yet "when he was abused, he did not return abuse." Isaiah wrote:

> Like a lamb that is led to the slaughter,
> and like a sheep that before its shearers is silent,
> so he did not open his mouth. (Isaiah 53:7)

In the words of the African American spiritual, "They crucified my Lord, and he never said a mumbalin' word, not a word, not a word, not a word."[2] Their harsh, hateful words failed to provoke a retaliatory response.

"When he suffered, he did not threaten" (1 Peter 2:23). While Jesus suffered one indignity after another, he could have appealed to God and instantly twelve legions of angels would have come to his defense (Matthew 26:53). Yet he never even threatened to use the power at his disposal. Unlike many celebrated Jewish martyrs, he did not rail against his executioners about the wrath God was storing up for them.

"But he entrusted himself to the one who judges justly" (1 Peter 2:23). Instead of retaliating, Jesus was content to commit his case to God. New Testament scholar Howard Marshall observes, "He left his destiny in the hands of God and obeyed the principle that a person should not seek revenge but rather leave the judgment of one's opponents to God."[3]

Having described the example Jesus left us by patiently enduring unjust suffering, Peter shifts directions. With Isaiah 53 still in the back of his mind, he goes on to describe the purpose of Christ's suffering for humanity in general.

"He himself bore our sins in his body on the cross" (1 *Peter* 2:24). Christ's death provided an example of suffering for us, but even more than that, it accomplished atonement for sin. New Testament scholar J. N. D. Kelly says, " 'Bearing sins' means taking the blame for sins, accepting the punishment due them, and so securing their putting away."[4] As he hung on the cross, Jesus took on himself the punishment for our sins.

However, through his sacrificial death, he did more than set us free from the negative consequences of our past sins. Once again echoing Isaiah, Peter goes on to spell out three positive benefits of the cross for our lives now:

1. Righteous living: "So that, free from sins, we might live for righteousness" (2:24).

2. Healing: "By his wounds you have been healed" (2:24).

3. Restoration: "For you were going astray like sheep, but now you have returned to the shepherd and guardian of your souls" (2:25).

On the cross Jesus opened up the possibility of new life—righteousness, healing and restoration—for his enemies and for all of humanity. Of course, his enemies were totally unaware of what he was doing. As their venomous curses poured out against him, all the while he was blessing them as he prayed, "Father, forgive them, for they know not what they do." He also promised salvation to the penitent thief hanging next to him: "Truly I tell you, today you will be with me in Paradise" (Luke 23:43). Jesus' words from the cross demonstrate his desire to bestow the blessings of forgiveness and eternal life on all.

In the light of how Christ loved his enemies, Peter later exhorts all

Christians encountering evil and unjust suffering: "Do not repay evil for evil or abuse for abuse; but, on the contrary, repay with a blessing. It is for this that you were called—that you might inherit a blessing" (1 Peter 3:9). Christ's example on the cross in bearing evil and blessing evildoers becomes the basis for what we are commanded to do in relation to those who have injured us.

BEARING EVIL

What does bearing evil mean in practical terms? How, for example, do sexual abuse victims bear the evil done to them and bless their abusers? How does a person who has gone through a painful divorce love a malicious ex-spouse? Romans 12:14-21 will help us find answers to these questions.

I want to begin by stressing that bearing evil doesn't mean disregarding or glossing over the evil done to us. In the last chapter we stressed that the first step in forgiving is facing the facts, being ruthlessly honest about wrongs done to us. The same applies here. Loving those who have hurt us may mean patiently bearing the wrongs they have done, but it doesn't mean ignoring or excusing what they've done.

In Romans 12:14-21, Paul makes two statements with regard to evil: "Do not repay anyone evil for evil" (v. 17), and "Do not be overcome by evil, but overcome evil with good" (v. 21). We'll consider what both of these verses mean, but first, notice what Paul says a few verses earlier: "Let love be genuine; *hate what is evil*, hold fast to what is good" (v. 9, emphasis mine). In addition to not repaying evil and to overcoming evil, we are told to hate evil.

But how can we love our enemies and hate their evil at the same time? Aren't the two mutually exclusive? Doesn't the presence of love expel hate and vice versa? Not according to Paul. He exhorts us to *both* love and hate. In fact, we could infer from his words that in order for love to be genuine, we must hate evil. John Stott's comment on this verse is insightful: "Whenever love is 'sincere' (literally, 'without hypocrisy'), it is morally discerning. It never pretends that evil is anything else or condones it. Compromise with evil is incompatible with love. Love seeks the highest good of others and therefore hates the evil that spoils it. God hates evil because his love is holy love; we must hate it too."[5]

Hating evil includes the yearning to see evildoers someday judged for their actions. As I said in the previous chapter, the longing to see righteousness, goodness and beauty prevail in our world has been planted in our hearts by God. The passion for legitimate vengeance is also part of that God-given desire. Many Christians consider any desire for vengeance as inherently evil. But God says, "Vengeance is mine, I will repay" (Romans 12:19; Deuteronomy 32:35). If vengeance is always wrong, how can God claim a right to it?

Of course, the way we humans express vengeance is often grievously wrong. It can flow out of the basest of motives, but vengeance in itself is not inherently evil; it's only evil when it takes the wrong form and is carried out at the wrong time. In their profound book *Bold Love,* Dan Allender and Tremper Longman III express this distinction well:

> Vengeance, at times, can be illegitimate, but it is not inherently wrong. Vengeance is part of the character of God and is not in contradiction with His love and mercy. Revenge involves a desire for justice. It is the intense wish to see ugliness destroyed, wrongs righted, and beauty restored. It is as inherent in the human soul as a desire for loveliness.[6]

Loving our enemies by bearing evil doesn't mean we tolerate the wrong they have inflicted on us and others. Love does not *condone* evil; rather, love *condemns* it, hates it for marring God's good creation and longs for the day of final reckoning and restoration. However, longing for that day doesn't give us the right to usher it in.

Paul's two other exhortations with regard to evil make that clear.

"Do not repay anyone evil for evil, but take thought for what is noble in the sight of all (12:17)." Paul's words, like Peter's (1 Peter 3:9), echo what Jesus says in the Sermon on the Mount: "Do not resist an evildoer" (Matthew 5:39). All three stress that bearing evil means refusing to retaliate. When we retaliate, we only add to the evil in the world. We fuel the fire of what Martin Luther King Jr. called "the chain reaction of evil." He says in his book *Strength to Love,* "Returning hate for hate multiplies hate, adding deeper darkness to a night already devoid of stars. Darkness cannot drive out darkness; only light can do that. Hate cannot drive out hate; only love can do that. Hate multiplies hate, violence multiplies violence, and toughness multiplies toughness in a descending spiral of destruction."[7]

When we repay evil with evil, not only do we increase evil, we also allow ourselves to be controlled by it. The evil done to us dictates our response. As a result, we become like the person we despise. Virgil Elizondo states that "the ultimate sinfulness of sin itself and its greatest tragedy is that it converts the victim into a sinner."[8]

When we refuse to retaliate, we break the chain reaction of evil in the world, and we also lessen evil's influence in our own lives. At times not retaliating may seem impractical or outrageous. Often we will fail to live up to such a lofty ideal, yet it is vital for our own spiritual survival. Every time we are able to refrain from retaliation, we demonstrate that God, not the power of evil, reigns in our life.

Although the desire for revenge is not inherently evil, acting on that desire by assuming the role of executioner is strictly forbidden in the Bible. Paul says, "Beloved, never avenge yourselves" (Romans 12:19). Loving our enemies means revoking our right to revenge. Instead we are to "leave room for the wrath of God; for it is written, 'Vengeance is mine, I will repay,' says the Lord" (Romans 12:19). To execute vengeance is unequivocally outside of human jurisdiction. It is God's prerogative, never ours. Only God knows everything necessary to justly and properly execute vengeance. We may groan with all creation (Romans 8:22-23) for the day of final redemption. With the martyred saints we may cry out, "How long will it be before you judge and avenge our blood?" (Revelation 6:9-11). But we must never take vengeance into our own hands; it must be left to God alone.

BLESSING THE EVILDOER

Having told us what not to do—retaliate or seek revenge—Paul, in his final exhortation, calls us to positive action: "Do not be overcome by evil, but overcome evil with good" (Romans 12:21). Evil can be overcome, conquered here and now, when we respond to it with good.

But what concrete expression should goodness take? Paul has already indicated two such expressions in the preceding verses. Echoing Jesus' words in the Sermon on the Mount (Matthew 5:44; Luke 6:27-28), he writes, "Bless those who persecute you; bless and do not curse them"(Romans 12:14). He also quotes from Proverbs: If your enemies are hungry, feed them; if they are thirsty, give them something to drink; for by doing this you will heap burning coals on their heads" (Romans 12:20; cf. Proverbs 25:21-22).

Doing good to those who have done evil to us involves both *words* and *deeds*, both *blessing* and *serving*. John Stott says, "In the new community of Jesus curses are to be replaced by blessings, malice by prayer, and revenge by service. In fact, prayer purges the heart of malice; the lips which bless cannot simultaneously curse; and the hand occupied with service is restrained from taking revenge."[9]

We need to be clear, however, that in practice, overcoming evil with good will often involve a toughness which runs counter to our sentimentalized conceptions of goodness. For truly doing good to someone will mean giving them what they most need—not necessarily what they want. For example, doing good to an angry, dictatorial father who insists on controlling his adult children may mean standing up to him and refusing to give in to his demands. On the other hand, in the case of a weak, indecisive mother, doing good may mean refusing to do anything in order to force her to make decisions on her own. As Allender and Longman suggest, "In many cases, [such] bold love will unnerve, offend, hurt, disturb, and compel the one who is loved to deal with the internal disease that is robbing him and others of joy."[10]

Such tough love is exemplified in the the last phrase of the passage Paul quotes from Proverbs. By giving food and drink to your enemy, it says, "you will heap burning coals on their heads" (Romans 12:20). Though to us it sounds like an unfriendly act, in biblical times this was a figure of speech for causing your enemies to feel a deep sense of shame, not in order to offend or humiliate them but to lead them to repentance and reconciliation.

Returning good for evil often surprises and stuns our enemies. They expect us to retaliate by resorting to the same power, manipulation and shaming tactics they use. The stark contrast between their action and our response disconcerts and unsettles them because it exposes the evil of what they have done. Yet the unwelcome exposure is actually a gracious gift to them. At first it may evoke shame, but it offers them an opportunity for self-examination and repentance. One way or another, it will cause them to change, either by softening their hearts or hardening them even more.

Dan Allender tells of a woman who suspected her husband of having an affair. One evening she flew to the city where he was supposed to be conducting a business meeting and checked in to the same hotel where he was staying. She waited and watched as later he and another woman entered his room and stayed together all night.

The next morning she went to the hotel dining room and walked up to the table where her husband and the woman were eating breakfast. After greeting her husband and introducing herself to the woman, she said, "We have a lot to talk about, but this may not be a very good time. Why don't the two of you decide when we could talk. I'll wait in my room for your response. Enjoy your breakfast."

Even though she was in terrible pain, she tried not to be hostile or vindictive. Neither did she ignore the harm or encourage the affair. Above all, she wanted to create an opportunity for God's grace to work in her husband's heart.

Later when he came alone to her room, she greeted him warmly but made it clear that their marriage was over unless he was willing to deal with the physical, emotional and spiritual violation of their covenant. Although she never threatened or harangued, she was lovingly forceful. Allender sums up the impact her enemy love had on her husband:

> He was stunned—almost to a point of inarticulate madness. She had never flown by herself or stayed in a hotel alone in her life. She was a dependent and frightened woman in most situations, yet she won over fear and loneliness and the shame and rage of facing her husband's lover. And of all things, she not only gave her husband the freedom to divorce her, but insisted he do so if he was unwilling to change. No greater gift of grace could have been offered and no greater slap endured than the manner in which she shamed her husband and received him back, if he chose to repent.[11]

This is the kind of radical love for our enemies to which we are called.

GOD'S WAY WILL WORK

Of course, when most of us are confronted with Christ's call to love our enemies, our initial reaction is negative. It seems preposterous, irrelevant, pathetic, noble perhaps, but definitely impractical. Yet as Jacob DeShazer says, "God's way *will work* if we will try it out. Jesus was not an idealist whose ideals could not be realized. When He told us to love one another, He told us the best way to act, and it will work."[12]

DeShazer is a living witness of how the power of Christ can enable us to love our enemies. Although emotional injury is not the primary focus of his story, I believe it will inspire you as you open yourself to Christ's command to love your enemies.

After Japan's attack on Pearl Harbor in December 1941, DeShazer, a bombardier in the U.S. Army, was consumed with such hate for the Japanese that he volunteered for a secret mission with the Jimmy Doolittle Squadron. Five months later, on April 18, 1942, the mission was carried out. It was a surprise bombing raid on Tokyo, launched from the aircraft carrier *Hornet*, and the bombs fell right on target. But unfortunately, several of the B-25s, including number 16, DeShazer's plane, ran out of fuel on route back to the carrier, and those on board were forced to parachute into Japanese territory. A few days later they were captured and imprisoned.

The Japanese were furious about the bombing and were determined to make their captives pay. They tied them to chairs and kicked their legs until their prisoners wondered if they'd ever walk again. One of the lieutenants was handcuffed, hoisted to a peg on the wall and left to hang there for more than eight hours. Another man had towels thrown over his face while the Japanese poured water over his nose and mouth until he nearly suffocated. Finally, after days of torture and interrogation, they threw them all into solitary cells.

In his cell, DeShazer's hatred for the Japanese festered. One day when the prison guard ordered him to clean up his cell, he refused. The enraged guard struck his head with his fist. DeShazer kicked him in the stomach. The guard drew his scabbard and began whipping his prisoner. But somehow the POW managed to reach a bucket of dirty mop water. He picked it up and threw it in his enemy's face. Stunned, the guard stood there, the suds dripping down his uniform. He hated DeShazer, DeShazer hated him, and it remained that way for the next two wretched years.

During those years the prisoners begged their captors for books.

Finally, in 1944 they were given a few, including a copy of the American Standard Version of the Bible. Each prisoner was allowed to keep it for three weeks. Although his parents were committed Christians and he had been raised in the church, DeShazer viewed Christianity as an angry and legalistic religion and had never been interested in the Bible before.

But when it was passed to him, encouraged by another prisoner who had been transformed as he read, DeShazer too found himself devouring it. As he studied, pondered and memorized the Scriptures, the written Word of God, DeShazer encountered Jesus Christ, the living Word of God. There in that dingy POW cell on June 8, 1944, he prayed to receive Christ and committed his life and his future to him. For the first time in over two years he was joyful.

As he immersed himself in Scripture, he was gripped by the strong emphasis on love in the New Testament. Since God loves us, it said, we are to love one another—including our enemies. But the idea of loving his Japanese captors seemed ludicrous to DeShazer. *Love them?* he thought. *You've got to be kidding.*

A few days later an incident occurred that revealed how difficult enemy love might be. DeShazer's guard was in a hurry to get him back into his cell. Opening the door, he shoved him inside. Before DeShazer was completely inside, he slammed the door and caught one of his feet. The guard began kicking DeShazer's bare foot with his hobnailed boot. Finally DeShazer was able to shove the door open and get his foot free. Resentment and hatred toward the guard welled up within him. He wanted to curse him, but then he remembered the words of Jesus in the Sermon on the Mount: "Love your enemies and pray for those who persecute you" (Matthew 5:44).

DeShazer had memorized the entire Sermon on the Mount, but he wanted to expunge that verse. Certainly Jesus didn't expect him to love someone who had just smashed his foot. Yet would God have given the command if it were impossible to obey? And hadn't he promised he would obey God no matter what? DeShazer made up his mind to try.

The next morning, when the guard came on duty, he limped to his cell door and instead of scowling, greeted him warmly. The guard was puzzled. For the next few days he ignored DeShazer's friendly overtures. Eventually, however, the two men began to talk. The guard was pleased because DeShazer wanted to know about his family. Later he began to bring his prisoner gifts—a boiled sweet potato, figs and candy. Even the other guards noticed DeShazer's changed attitude. "Number five is the nicest one," they remarked to one another.

A year later in August 1945, as the war drew to a close, DeShazer's love for his enemies intensified. For several days as he lay on the mat in his cell, his soul was flooded with waves of divine love. As he described it, "I felt love toward the Japanese people and a deep interest in their welfare. I felt that we were all made by the same God and that we must share our hardships and our happiness together. How I wished I could tell the Japanese people about Jesus! I knew that my Savior would be their Savior too."[3] Ten days later, on August 20, 1945, after forty months of imprisonment, DeShazer and the other POWs walked free and returned home to America.

A few years later, DeShazer's prayer for the Japanese people was answered. In December 1948, he sailed for Japan to serve as a missionary there for the Free Methodist Church. Before his retirement, he and his wife, Florence, spent over thirty years ministering in Japan and introducing thousands of Japanese to new life in Christ.

DeShazer's story first appeared in a leaflet, *I Was a Prisoner of Japan*, which contributed to the conversion of many, including Captain Mitsuo Fuchida who had commanded the Japanese air squadron that bombed Pearl Harbor. Reading DeShazer's testimony in October 1948 prompted Fuchida to buy a Bible. When he opened it nine months later, he was gripped by its message and especially

Christ's prayer from the cross, "Father, forgive them; for they do not know what they are doing" (Luke 23:34). He wept as he realized Christ had prayed and died for him. In September 1949, Fuchida received Christ as Savior and Lord, and he was baptized on Easter Sunday in 1951. In later years, DeShazer and Fuchida often joined together to witness and preach to overflow crowds in Japan and abroad.

"Love your enemies." It seems ridiculous and impractical. But as DeShazer discovered, "God's way *will work* if we will try it out." As we do, we will discover, as he did, that as Christ commands us to act, so he enables us. He never asks us to do anything without providing the power to do it. As we choose to love our enemies, Christ's love for them will be imparted to us.

Are we willing then to try? Are we willing to allow Christ to remove the obstacles to loving our enemies that are lodged in our hearts? Are we willing to let go of our resentment and bitterness, our desire for retaliation and revenge? And are we willing to allow Christ to actually place within us a love for our enemies that will seek to bless them?

At the conclusion of *People of the Lie*, his profound book on evil, Scott Peck describes how amazing things happen when Christ is allowed to transform our hearts so that his love for our enemies can flow from them. Peck maintains that this is the only way evil can be overcome. Consider his moving description of the transformation that can occur in us:

> When one has purified oneself, by the grace of God, to the point at which one can truly love one's enemies, a beautiful thing happens. It is as if the boundaries of the soul become so clean as to be transparent, and a unique light then shines forth from the individual. . . .
>
> The healing of evil—scientifically or otherwise—can be ac-

complished only by the love of individuals. A willing sacrifice is required. The individual healer must allow his or her own soul to become the battleground. He or she must sacrificially *absorb* the evil. . . .

I do not know how this occurs. But I know that it does. I know that good people can deliberately allow themselves to be pierced by the evil of others—to be broken thereby and somehow not broken—to even be killed in some sense and yet still survive and not succumb. Whenever this happens there is a slight shift in the balance of power in the world.[4]

Will we let this happen in us? Will we let ourselves become a willing sacrifice? Will we allow our own souls to become the battleground? To become a channel of love flowing out to someone who has wounded us deeply?

Christ can fill our hearts with such love. It happens slowly as we take one tiny step at a time toward enemy love. But when we seek to obey his command to love our enemies, he accomplishes this good work in us. Good will overcome evil, and the world's balance of power will have shifted.

QUESTIONS FOR PERSONAL OR GROUP REFLECTION

1. Have you ever seriously tried to obey Christ's command to "love your enemies"? What particular attitudes and actions toward your enemy did that involve? What happened as a result?

2. Instead of retaliating, Jesus was content to commit his case to God. He loved his enemies by bearing sin and opening up the possibility of new life—righteousness, healing and restoration— for them and for all humanity. What aspect of Jesus' example of enemy loving evokes the greatest response from you?

3. Is there anyone toward whom you harbor a desire for revenge?

What makes it difficult to release that to God?

4. What specific loving actions might God be asking you to take toward someone you consider an enemy?

5. Are you willing to allow Christ to remove the obstacles to "enemy-loving" lodged in your heart? Are you willing to let go of resentment and bitterness, your desire for retaliation and revenge? And are you willing to allow Christ to actually place within you a love for your enemies that will seek to bless them?

Let these questions and their answers forge a prayer that will allow the river of God's love to flow into the parched land of your soul.

Radiant Scars

How splendid the cross of Christ!
It brings life, not death;
Light not darkness; Paradise, not its loss.
It is the wood on which
The Lord, like a great warrior,
Was wounded in hands and feet and side,
But healed thereby our wounds
A tree had destroyed us;
A tree now brought us life.

SAINT THEODORE OF STUDIOS

The March 27, 2000, issue of *Newsweek* featured as its cover story an article titled "Visions of Jesus: How Jews, Muslims and Buddhists View Him." Though people practicing these religions do not consider Christ to be the unique Son of God, as Christians do, the article showed how greatly Jesus is revered and admired in all the world's major religions.

Muslims, for example, recognize Jesus as a great prophet. They even believe he was born of a virgin and ascended into heaven, spiritual prerogatives not even belonging to Muhammad, whom they consider the greatest of all their prophets. Jews have gained greater admiration for Jesus in recent centuries, viewing him as a reformer within Judaism who sought to liberalize his own religious tradition. In their view, Jesus' followers mistakenly went on to worship him and establish a new religion, something Jesus himself never intended. At some Jewish seminaries, a course in the New Testament is even required of rabbinical candidates.

Although they find his notion of a single god unnecessarily restrictive, Hindus also view Jesus as a virtuous man. Like Mahatma Gandhi, many Hindus are drawn to Jesus because of his compassion for others and his commitment to nonviolence. Some even maintain that when Jesus was a teenager he journeyed to India where he learned Hindu meditation and then later returned to Palestine and became a Jewish guru.

Buddhists are quick to point out similarities between the stories of Jesus and Buddha. One Zen Buddhist monk maintains Jesus and Buddha are "brothers" who both taught that the highest form of human understanding is universal love. Many Buddhists regard Jesus, like Buddha, as a perfectly enlightened being who sought to help others find enlightenment.

Yet having clearly shown the universal appeal of Jesus by observing him in the mirrors of Jews and Muslims, Hindus and Buddhists, the article reached an unexpected conclusion. Instead of suggesting that the universal admiration of Jesus may serve as a bridge in uniting Christianity with the other major world religions, it focused on the central element in the Christian view of Jesus that creates a stumbling block for them all: his violent death on the cross. As the article put it:

> Clearly, the cross is what separates the Christ of Christianity from every other Jesus. In Judaism there is no precedent for a Messiah who dies, much less as a criminal as Jesus did. In Islam, the story of Jesus' death is rejected as an affront to Allah himself. Hindus can accept only a Jesus who passes into peace-

ful samadhi, a yogi who escapes the degradation of death. The figure of the crucified Christ, says Buddhist Thich Nhat Hanh, "is a very painful image to me. It does not contain joy or peace, and this does not do justice to Jesus." There is, in short, no room in other religions for a Christ who experiences the full burden of mortal existence—and hence there is no reason to believe in him as the divine Son whom the Father resurrects from the dead.[1]

Attributing crucial significance to Christ's agonizing, shameful death is unique to Christianity. Unlike other world religions, which reject or downplay his death, Christians do the opposite. In our theology, worship, preaching, art, hymnody and architecture, we celebrate, lift high, even *glory* in the cross. From the second century onward, not only have Christians drawn, painted and engraved the cross as the central pictorial symbol of their faith, they also make the sign of the cross on themselves and others. Around A.D. 200, Tertullian, a North African theologian, described Christian practice like this: "At every forward step and movement, at every going in and out, when we put on our clothes and shoes, when we bathe, when we sit at table, when we light the lamps, on couch, on seat, in all the ordinary actions of daily life, we trace upon the forehead the sign [the cross]."[2] What the irreligious and those of other religions find contradictory, bewildering and offensive, Christians, in stark contrast, consider essential, indispensable and precious.

In the Christian scheme of things, even after Christ was raised from the dead and given a glorious new resurrection body, the scars in his hands and feet and side—emblems of his gruesome death—remain. God's power overcame all other evidence of violence done to him. Suffering and death were left behind; he was alive as never before. Yet these marks of humiliation were not erased. In fact, his scars became his identifying marks. On that first Easter when his disciples were hiding behind closed doors, he appeared among them and "showed them his hands and his side." Then they absolutely knew it was Jesus and "rejoiced when they saw the Lord" (John 20:20).

Edward Shillito's poem "Jesus of the Scars" was inspired by these words from John's Gospel. Written in the aftermath of the destruction and carnage of World War I, it witnesses to the comfort and hope the marks of Christ's crucifixion continue to bring to his followers:

> If we have never sought, we seek Thee now;
>   Thine eyes burn through the dark, our only stars;
> We must have sight of thorn-pricks on Thy brow,
>   We must have Thee, O Jesus of the Scars.
>
> The heavens frighten us; they are too calm;
>   In all the universe we have no place.
> Our wounds are hurting us; where is the balm?
>   Lord Jesus, by Thy Scars, we claim Thy grace.
>
> If, when the doors are shut, Thou drawest near,
>   Only reveal those hands, that side of Thine;
> We know today what wounds are, have no fear,
>   Show us Thy Scars, we know the countersign.
>
> The other gods were strong; but Thou wast weak;
>   They rode, but Thou didst stumble to a throne;
> But to our wounds only God's wounds can speak,
>   And not a god has wounds, but Thou alone.[3]

Christians have always looked to the scars and always will. Throughout eternity we will gather around the throne of God and sing about the glories of the Lamb who was slain (Revelation 5:8-14).

GOD'S MEANS OF REDEMPTION

Why is it that Christians *glory* in the cross? Why do they pray, with Shillito, "We must have thee, O Jesus of the scars"? While every other religion is repulsed by Christ's suffering and death, why do Christians rejoice over them? Because we believe the cross is God's supreme instrument in redeeming fallen creation.

We believe God's solution to the problem of suffering and evil is not to eliminate it, nor to be insulated from it, but to participate in it and then, having participated in it, to transform it into his instrument for redeeming the world. This is what Simone Weil meant when she said, "The extreme greatness of Christianity lies in the fact that it does not seek a supernatural remedy for suffering but a supernatural use for it."[4] Rather than hindering God's work, suffering and evil actually weave into God's redemptive plan and pattern for the salvation of the world. God takes terrible tragedy and turns it into triumph; the grotesque becomes glorious, evil is transmuted into good. Emil Brunner is right: "If there ever were an event in which evil, innocent suffering, malice and human pain reaches its climax, it is in the cross of Christ."[5] Yet God took the awfulness of that event—the diabolical evil, the flagrant injustice, the excruciating pain—mixed them together and, through a marvelous divine alchemy, transformed them into medicine for the healing of the nations.

The cross profoundly illustrates Romans 8:28: "We know that all things work together for good for those who love God, who are called according to his purpose." It demonstrates that even when things seem to have gone tragically wrong, God can still use anguish creatively to bring out of it blessings that could not have been realized any other way. In fact, this *is* God's method of redemption; this is how God, in the face of evil, works to accomplish his will and purpose in the world.

How does God overcome that which opposes his will? How does God demonstrate divine sovereignty and power in the face of evil? The cross tells us: God accomplishes it through a power that absorbs opposition to his will through innocent suffering and then, having absorbed the opposition, neutralizes it by forgiving love. Finally, having neutralized evil, God uses it to accomplish the very purpose it was originally designed to thwart.

God overcomes evil not through passive resignation or brute strength, not through coercion or a dazzling display of force, but through the power of suffering love. God uses suffering redemptively to accomplish his will and purpose in the world. That's why Christ's scars are still there even when he returns with a glorified body after his triumphant resurrection. And they will always be there, but with one crucial difference: now they are radiant scars. A verse in the hymn "Crown Him with Many Crowns" conveys this so beautifully: "Crown him the Lord of love; behold his hands and side, those wounds, yet visible above, in beauty glorified." The scars are now bearers of divine glory, radiating the light of God's presence, which transforms everything it encounters. His scars are now instruments of healing. As the Scripture says, "By his wounds we are healed" (Isaiah 53:5 NIV).

STRENGTH MADE PERFECT IN WEAKNESS

In the last three chapters, we have considered what the cross tells us about healing our emotional hurts. We can sum up the message of those chapters in three words: *embracing, forgiving, loving.* The cross reveals that healing comes through embracing, not avoiding, the pain of our hurts; through forgiving, not resenting, those who have wronged us; and through loving, not hating, those who have treated us like enemies. Now in the light of Christ's radiant scars we must add a fourth word: *offering.* Healing comes as we offer our wounds to God to be used as instruments in God's service for the redeeming of ourselves and others.

A woman at a summer camp in Canada where I was speaking shared how God was teaching her this. "Just a few weeks ago," she began, "my husband and I made a compost pile. We put all sorts of garbage in it—cracked eggshells, darkened banana peels, coffee grinds, piles of rotten leaves and grass—you name it. We mixed it all together and then covered it up. And when you go near it now, believe me, your nose knows it's there! But next spring when we use it in our garden and around our shrubs, what's decaying garbage now will be pure gold. That compost will be so much better than any fertilizer we could buy at the store."

Then she made this application to herself: "There has been lots of garbage in my life—rotten things done to me and rotten things I've done in response. For years I refused to deal with the garbage, but several years ago when my life began to unravel, I was forced to. Thank God for that. As a result, he has worked so much healing and restoration in my life.

"But while all this has been going on, I have often found myself thinking, *I can't wait until this is finally over. I'll be so glad when I can put all the garbage behind me and never have to think about it again. Maybe I'll even be able to pretend it never happened.*

"Then as we were making the compost pile the Lord spoke to me: 'All your life you've run from your garbage. Now even though you're finally dealing with it and receiving healing, you still want to run from it. But don't you see? I not only want to heal and free you from its effects in your life, I want to use your garbage. Like the garbage in your compost pile, if you'll let me, I'll turn it into pure gold. I'll use it to build character in you and bring healing and freedom to others.'

"So instead of being ashamed of the garbage, I'm learning to give it to him. And I'm discovering the Lord is the great Recycler! He doesn't waste anything. He can turn our garbage into gold—pure gold, if we'll just offer it to him."

The apostle Paul shares a similar message in his second letter to the Corinthians, where he writes candidly about a "thorn . . . in the flesh" (12:7), with which he had to contend. *Skolops*, the Greek word for "thorn," can mean either a stake that actually pegged a person to the ground or a splinter that was constantly irritating. According to

H. Minn, it conveyed "the notion of something sharp and painful which sticks deep in the flesh and in the will of God defies extraction. The effect of its presence was to cripple Paul's enjoyment of life, and to frustrate his full efficiency by draining his energies."[6]

Scholars have conjectured about the exact nature of Paul's "thorn." Was it a particular person who relentlessly opposed Paul, persecution in general, a besetting sin or temptation, a speech impediment or a physical infirmity such as epilepsy or an eye disorder? All have been suggested. The fact that Paul doesn't specify, however, has made this passage an even greater blessing to Christians. They have been able to apply what he says to various kinds of "thorns" in their lives, including those resulting from emotional wounds.

It is significant that Paul refers to his thorn as "a messenger of Satan to torment me" (2 Corinthians 12:7). He recognized its evil nature, something that was intended to thwart God's purposes for him. At first, he vigorously and persistently prayed for its removal: "Three times I appealed to the Lord about this, that it would leave me" (2 Corinthians 12:8).

In light of Paul's prayer, it would therefore seem right for us to intently pray for healing of our emotional hurts and for their total removal. No doubt that is God's ultimate will. For there will come a day when

> he will wipe every tear from [our] eyes. . . .
> Mourning and crying and pain will be no more.
> (Revelation 21:4)

By praying for complete healing, we exercise faith that it will be so. And—praise God—there are times when God can and does heal by complete removal and deliverance. For some, what will be true for all believers in the future age miraculously breaks into the present.

But that's not how Paul's prayer was answered. His thorn was not taken away. Instead, he heard the Lord say, "My grace is sufficient for you, for power is made perfect in weakness" (2 Corinthians 12:9). God's response to Paul's thorn was not to remove it but to give Paul grace to endure and to use Paul's resulting weakness as an opportunity to demonstrate divine power. Just as Christ himself was "crucified in weakness" (2 Corinthians 13:4), and his weakness in death demonstrated the power of God (1 Corinthians 1:22-25), Paul's thorn-related weakness produced similar results. There is no doubt that God could have demonstrated his power by removing Paul's thorn. But by not removing it, God chose to do something even better: to perfect his power through weakness.

As a result, Paul's attitude toward his thorn was transformed. Instead of letting the presence of the thorn fuel anger or self-pity, Paul boasted in the weakness caused by the thorn. He exclaims, "So, I will boast all the more gladly of my weaknesses, so that the power of Christ may dwell in me" (2 Corinthians 12:9). Contrary to what we would think, Paul's thorn-produced weakness didn't create frustration and dissatisfaction in him. Instead it led to contentment: "Therefore, I am content with weaknesses," he declares, for he realizes that "whenever I am weak, then I am strong" (2 Corinthians 12:10).

HOW OUR SCARS BECOME RADIANT

Is it possible for us to come to the place where we can view our emotional scars the way Paul looked at his thorn? I believe we can eventually, but not at the beginning of the healing process. At that point our most crucial task is to embrace the pain, confront the truth and come to terms with the havoc wreaked in our lives by our hurts. As we honestly and carefully survey the damage, taking the first steps toward healing requires that we view our hurts as evil—messengers of Satan sent to destroy us—and therefore as enemies to be fought against and overcome.

But there comes a point in the healing process where we are called to face our wounds in a different way, viewing them this time not as enemies but as friends. While recognizing their evil intent, we actually come to glory in them like Paul did, because of what they produce *in* us (weakness) and consequently what they release *through* us (God's power). Alexander MacClaren, a twentieth-century Scottish preacher, said, "Don't seek to be an iron pillar. Iron pillars are not useful to God. God uses broken reeds." God builds his kingdom on human weakness, not human strength.

Of course, such a notion stands in direct contradiction to our pride and perfectionism. Who wants to be a broken reed? We would prefer God minimize our weaknesses and magnify our strengths. But in God's kingdom everything is turned upside down. Strength is made perfect in weakness.

I once read a story about a woman traveling on an interstate highway, sitting in the back of the car looking out the window. The sun shone brightly, revealing all the window's flaws and scratches. As the woman fastened her eyes on one particular scratch, the perfectionist in her was annoyed. *This window is no good*, she thought. *It ought to be replaced. What an awful scratch.*

However, a moment later she noticed something else. The sunlight reflecting through the scratch had fashioned a tiny but exquisite rainbow. *I can focus on the scratch*, she thought, *or I can focus on the rainbow.* She decided for the rainbow.

When we consider the scratches on the windows of our souls, like the woman, our first response is to pray, "What a mess! Lord, get rid of them. Then I'll be able to serve you well." But God's ways are different from ours. God wants to use our scratches to refract his light into rainbows, to use our anguish to create beauty that couldn't be produced any other way.

Don Crossland tells about a time he was addressing a group of two hundred men. Because of his insecurity and need to be accepted, he at first tried to impress his audience by describing the successful church he once pastored. Then he found himself "name dropping" by talking about his relationships with several professional football players. As he was speaking, however, the Spirit began to prompt him to humble himself and talk openly about some of his hurts and fears. At first he resisted, but then he hesitantly obeyed. Don told them about some of his unmet needs for love and how his efforts to fulfill them had led to sexual and emotional addiction. He wasn't sure how the men would respond to his honesty, but when he was finished, so many came forward in response to his invitation that there wasn't time to minister to them all.

That day he learned about Christ's strength perfected in his weakness—a pattern that continues in his ministry. He says:

> Interestingly, despite all my years of leading a successful church ministry, I have never been asked to speak on church growth. What God has used most in my life is not what I would have considered my strengths and successes. Instead, it has been out of my failures that the love and power of Jesus Christ have been revealed. When people look at me, they do not glory in my strength, but they glory in the power and majesty of God's grace in my life.[7]

Are we willing to let the Lord glorify himself with our wounds?

As I was praying with a sexual abuse victim, she heard Jesus speak these words to her: "The channels which have been cut into your soul will release joy." He was assuring her that her deep wounds, like his, would one day become wounds that heal. Yet as she continues to press into painful memories of abuse, she struggles with this notion. The thought that someday God may be calling her to a ministry with sexual abuse victims makes her shudder, stirring up the unresolved emotional pain within her.

You may be at a similar place in your healing journey. You may have come a long way in embracing the pain, forgiving those who wounded you, even loving those who have treated you like enemies.

Consequently, significant levels of healing have occurred; dimensions of freedom have emerged. Even if we're grateful for all Christ has done, the thought that God desires to use our wounds, that our scars, like Christ's, can become radiant, is unwelcome, perhaps even repulsive. What then should we do?

Let me make two suggestions.

First, having honestly recognized we're not ready to offer our wounds to God to use, we must give God permission to bring us to that point. As I've stressed in relation to other steps in the healing process, the most important thing we can offer to God is our willingness. We will never overcome our resistance by talking ourselves out of it. Our scars are too deep for that. There is nothing we can do to effect this inner transformation. Jesus must do it. But he needs our permission; he won't work against our will. He needs our cooperation and our willingness before he will do this good work in us. So let's offer that to him. Paul was able to "glory in his weaknesses." We're not able to do that yet, but we can pray, "Lord, we want to be able to. We want to be able to glory in our weaknesses. We want you to use our wounds. You have permission to do whatever is necessary to bring us to the place where that can happen."

Second, we need to consider our scars in the light of Christ's radiant scars. Picture him standing before us as he stood before his disciples on that first Easter. Like he did then, he shows us the scars from the wounds he received on the cross. Now, however, light floods out from them, transforming everything it touches and filling them with life. As we gaze at his wounds and consider ours in relation to his, we can offer our wounds to him, asking him to touch them with his and to transform them into radiant scars.

A young woman who had been physically and emotionally abused by her parents shared with me a poem she had written, in which she reflected on her scars in the light of Christ's. She wrote:

The scars I wear—
I wish weren't there . . .
but with injury
such markings are made.

Marks embedded deep—
memories oft for keep . . .
for their origin
may still bring forth pain.

Some cover their scars—
or run off afar . . .
afraid to be seen;
they run for cover. . . .

The scars that Christ bears—
just marks that He cares . . .
not worn with pride
or hidden in shame.

Love grafted in hands—
stripes part of a plan . . .
imprints of beauty;
just marks in disguise.

My scars I can't hide—
though oft I have tried . . .
imprints of beauty;
just marks in disguise.

As we stand before Christ, gazing at his scars, allowing their radiance to penetrate ours, and as we offer our scars to him, the time will come time when we find ourselves saying about our scars what we say about his: "imprints of beauty, just marks in disguise."

I will never forget a seminary chapel service in May 2000 when

Mattie Greathouse, a graduating student, shared about how Christ had transformed her scars. Eight months after Mattie's birth, her father shot and killed her mother. Even though she was in denial about his violent act during her growing up years, its impact on her was profound: "That eerie, sketchy story hounded my childhood and adolescence. It was an identity I refused to acknowledge, but that wound and its implications were inescapable."

During her years at Asbury, however, she began to accept that story as her own. "The personal trauma that had been carefully stuffed for 27 years finally came out, and became mine."[8] A breakthrough occurred on the day she married Chad, a man she had met while in seminary.

Mattie had been adopted and raised by her maternal grandparents. Because of her father's violent act, all ties with his side of the family had been cut off. But as a result of owning what had been done to her, she felt nudged to invite her father's family to the wedding. At the reception she met her paternal grandmother, along with an aunt and uncle, for the first time.

The following summer she visited her father's extended family. She also visited her father himself in prison. There, for the first time, Mattie sat with the man who was instrumental of such great evil in her life.

Although she had forgiven her father, in her testimony Mattie was emphatic about the devastating effects of his evil act. "My father's sin, violence, and betrayal were no 'blessing in disguise.' God did not remove the sting of grief, anger or the other countless ramifications of my birth father's sins. His action was a curse. For many years the evil of that event bred all sorts of cancer in our family."[9]

However, Mattie was even more emphatic that where sin had abounded, God's grace had abounded even more (Romans 5:20). Christ had brought triumph out of her tragedy. In fact, the evil in her life by which she never wanted to be identified had become the supreme demonstration of his grace and power. As she so wonderfully expressed it, "Christ Jesus took that curse and blessed me, and is making me a blessing in the midst and even in spite of it. Indeed I am the genetic daughter of a murderer; but much more am I the ransomed, healed, restored and forgiven *adopted* daughter of the king of kings; sister of the prince of peace. My father's violence has not had the last word; evil has not ultimately triumphed."[10]

In reflecting on the mystery of evil in her life and the miracle Christ's triumph over it, Mattie concluded her testimony by pointing to the cross. There Christ's wounds and hers were somehow brought together. And there her scars, because of his, had somehow become radiant. "I do not fully know why I suffered this loss, nor why my birth father's injustice has scarred my face. However, I know the One who was scarred for me. When I break open the words of God to those who do not know Him, my own scars will testify to the reality of His grace—to His scars. Indeed 'by his wounds we are healed.'"[11]

Can you say that about your scars? If not, bring them to the cross. Let Christ's scars touch yours. In time your scars, too, will testify to the reality of his grace and to his scars. Yours too, like his, will become radiant.

QUESTIONS FOR PERSONAL OR GROUP REFLECTION

1. Like the garbage in a compost pile, God wants to turn our garbage into gold. In your "compost pile" of suffering and woundedness, what "fertile ground" for God's work is beginning to emerge?

2. Paul came to the place where he was able to boast about his weaknesses since they showed forth Christ's strength. Have you ever boasted about a weakness? Have you testified about God carrying you through situations that you could not overcome in your own strength? Are there struggles that you deal with a day at a time for which you need to appropriate God's sufficient strength?

3. What might be different in your attitude and in your self-esteem if you viewed your emotional wounds not simply as enemies but also as friends?

4. Is there anything that causes you hesitation about surrendering your scars to God? Are you willing to offer him those wounds, asking him to touch them with his own wounds and transform them into radiant scars?

Notes

Chapter 1: Bringing Our Hurts to the Cross

[1]Randy and Terry Butler, "At the Cross," Mercy/Vineyard Publishing, 1993.
[2]Quoted in Jürgen Moltmann, *The Crucified God* (New York: Harper & Row, 1974), p. 220.
[3]Frank Lake, *Clinical Theology* (London: Darton, Longman & Todd, 1966), p. 18.
[4]Ibid., p. 41.
[5]Franz Delitzsch, *Biblical Commentary on the Prophecies of Isaiah*, vol. 2, trans. James Martin (Grand Rapids, Mich.: Eerdmans, 1950), p. 316.
[6]Quoted in Lake, *Clinical Theology*, p. 13.
[7]George A. Buttrick, *Jesus Came Preaching* (New York: C. Scribner's Sons, 1932), p. 207.
[8]Joni Eareckson Tada, *Christian Counseling Connection*, vol. 3, ed. Gary Collins (Glen Ellyn, Ill.: Christian Counseling Resources, 1999).
[9]Dennis Ngien, "The God Who Suffers," *Christianity Today*, February 3, 1997, p. 42.
[10]Ibid.

Chapter 2: Despised and Rejected

[1]*Webster's New World Dictionary: Third College Edition* (New York: Simon & Schuster, 1991), p. 1132.
[2]Frank Lake, *Clinical Theology* (London: Darton, Longman & Todd, 1966), p. 1116.
[3]Leanne Payne, *Restoring the Christian Soul Through Healing Prayer* (Wheaton, Ill.: Crossway, 1991), pp. 93-94.
[4]Nancy Verrier, *The Primal Wound* (Baltimore: Gateway, 1997).
[5]Frank Lake, *Personal Identity—Its Origin* (Oxford: Clinical Theology Association, 1987), p. 6.
[6]Payne, *Restoring the Christian Soul*, p. 36.
[7]Henri Blocher, *Songs of the Servant* (Downers Grove, Ill.: InterVarsity Press, 1975), pp. 63-64.
[8]Lake, *Clinical Theology*, p. 1113.
[9]Philip Yancey, *The Jesus I Never Knew* (Grand Rapids, Mich.: Zondervan, 1995), p. 199.
[10]W. D. Edwards et al., "On the Physical Death of Jesus," *Journal of the American Medical Association* 255, no. 11 (1986): 1455-63.
[11]Ibid., p. 1457.

Chapter 3: Disregarding the Shame

[1]Quoted in Lewis Smedes, *Shame and Grace* (New York: HarperCollins, 1993), p. 95.
[2]John Bradshaw, *Healing the Shame That Binds You* (Deerfield Beach, Fla.: Health Communications, 1988), p. vii.
[3]Smedes, *Shame and Grace*, p.5.
[4]Robert Karen, "Shame," *The Atlantic Monthly* (February 1992): 42-43.
[5]Ibid., p. 47.
[6]Bradshaw, *Healing the Shame That Binds You*, p. 10
[7]Dan Allender and Tremper Longman III, *The Cry of the Soul* (Colorado Springs: NavPress, 1994), pp. 198-99.

[8]Martin Hengel, *Crucifixion in the Ancient World and the Folly of the Message of the Cross*, trans. John Bowden (Philadelphia: Fortress, 1977), p. 38.
[9]Quoted in Philip Yancey, *The Jesus I Never Knew* (Grand Rapids, Mich.: Zondervan, 1995), p. 200.
[10]Hengel, *Crucificxion in the Ancient World*, pp. 87-88.
[11]Quoted in Rodney Clapp, "Shame Crucified," *Christianity Today*, March 11, 1991, p. 28.
[12]Frank Lake, *Clinical Theology* (London: Darton, Longman & Todd, 1966), pp. 1114-15.
[13]David Seamands, *If Only* (Wheaton, Ill.: Victor, 1995), p. 60.
[14]Clapp, "Shame Crucified," p. 28.
[15]Heinrich Schlier, "Parrhesia," *Theological Dictionary of the New Testament*, ed. Gerhard Kittel and Gerhard Friedrich, trans. Geoffrey W. Bromiley (Grand Rapids, Mich.: Eerdmans, 1964), p. 883.

Chapter 4: Why Have You Forsaken Me?
[1]John Stott, *The Cross of Christ* (Downers Grove, Ill.: InterVarsity Press, 1986), p. 329.
[2]Pierre Wolff, *May I Hate God?* (New York: Paulist, 1979), p. 35.
[3]Ibid., p. 36.
[4]Ibid., p. 37.
[5]Jürgen Moltmann, *The Trinity and the Kingdom* (San Francisco: Harper & Row, 1981), p. 80.
[6]Fanny Crosby, "Rescue the Perishing," 1869.
[7]Frank Lake, *Clinical Theology* (London: Darton, Longman & Todd, 1966), p. 190.

Chapter 5: He Led Captivity Captive
[1]Gary Moon, *Homesick for Eden* (Ann Arbor, Mich.: Vine, 1997), p. 40.
[2]Ibid., p. 41.
[3]Ibid., pp. 42-43.
[4]Ibid.
[5]Ibid., p. 47.
[6]Patrick Carnes, *Out of the Shadows* (Minneapolis: CompCare Publications, 1983), p. vi.
[7]Don Crossland, *A Journey Toward Wholeness* (Nashville: StarSong Publishing, 1991), pp. 20-21.
[8]Stephen Arterburn, *Addicted to "Love"* (Ann Arbor, Mich.: Servant, 1991), p. 144.
[9]Ibid., pp. 137-38.
[10]Gerald May, *Addiction and Grace* (San Francisco: Harper & Row, 1988), pp. 26-30.
[11]Klaas Schilder, *Christ Crucified* (Grand Rapids, Mich.: Eerdmans, 1941), pp. 206-7.
[12]C. S. Lewis, *The Lion, the Witch and the Wardrobe* (New York: Collier, 1986), pp. 149-52.
[13]Ibid., p. 159.
[14]Quoted in Earl Jabay, *The Kingdom of Self* (Plainfield, N.J.: Logos International, 1974), pp. 58-59.
[15]Ted Roberts, *Pure Desire* (Ventura, Calif.: Regal, 1999), p. 128.
[16]Augustus Toplady, "Rock of Ages, Cleft for Me," 1776.

Chapter 6: Deliverance for Those Who Are Bound
[1]Charles Kraft, *Deep Wounds, Deep Healing* (Ann Arbor, Mich.: Servant, 1993), pp. 257-59.
[2]Terry Wardle, *Healing Care, Healing Prayer* (Orange, Calif.: New Leaf, 2001), p. 215.
[3]Among them are Merrill Unger, Michael Green, Kurt Koch, Mark Bubeck, Fred Dickason, Charles Kraft, Neil Anderson, Timothy Warner, Francis MacNutt, Tom White, Derek Prince, Terry Wardle, Ed Murphy and Clinton Arnold. Theologian Fred Dickason's 350-page book

Demon Possession and the Christian (Chicago: Moody Press, 1987) is the most exhaustive study on the subject. The most helpful concise treatment I have found is "Can a Christian Be Demon-Possessed?" chapter two in New Testament scholar Clinton Arnold's *Three Crucial Questions About Spiritual Warfare* (Grand Rapids, Mich.: Baker, 1997).
[4]Arnold, *Three Crucial Questions*, p. 79.
[5]Wardle, *Healing Care, Healing Prayer*, p. 221.
[6]Eduard Lohse, *Colossians and Philemon* (Philadelphia: Fortress, 1971), pp. 106-7.
[7]Quoted in Thomas Oden, *The Word of Life* (San Francisco: Harper & Row, 1989), p. 397.
[8]William F. Arndt and F. W. Gingrich, *A Greek-English Lexicon of the New Testament and Other Early Christian Literature* (Chicago: University of Chicago Press, 1957), p. 889.
[9]Peter O'Brien, *Colossians, Philemon* (Waco, Tex.: Word, 1982), p. 126.
[10]Michael Green, *I Believe in Satan's Downfall* (London: Hodder & Stoughton, 1981), pp. 214-15.
[11]Donald Demaray, *The Little Flowers of St. Francis: A Paraphrase* (New York: Alba House, 1992), pp. 85-86.

Chapter 7: Embracing the Pain

[1]Andrea Midgett, "Picturing the Cross," *Christianity Today*, April 3, 1995, p. 43.
[2]Klaas Schilder, *Christ Crucified* (Grand Rapids, Mich.: Eerdmans, 1940), pp. 98-99.
[3]Frank Lake, *Clinical Theology* (London: Darton, Longman & Todd, 1966), pp. xxx, xxii.
[4]Scott Peck, *The Road Less Traveled* (New York: Touchstone Books, 1978), pp. 16-17.
[5]Quoted in Gladys Hunt, "The Good of Suffering," *Christianity Today*, May 24, 1974, p. 36.
[6]Matt and Julie Woodley, *Restoring the Heart* (self-published pamphlet, 1999), p. 29.
[7]Dan Allender, *The Healing Path* (Colorado Springs: Waterbrook, 1999), p. 14.
[8]Hannah Hurnard, *Hinds' Feet on High Places* (Wheaton, Ill.: Tyndale House, 1986), p. 66.
[9]Ted Roberts, *Pure Desire* (Ventura, Calif.: Regal, 1999), pp. 181-82.
[10]Don Crossland, *A Journey Toward Wholeness* (Nashville: StarSong Publishing, 1991), p. 82.
[11]Woodley, *Restoring the Heart*, p. 30.
[12]Ibid.

Chapter 8: Father, Forgive Them

[1]Katherine Ann Birge, "How Come Jesus Got to Be so Great?" *The Living Pulpit* (April-June 1994): 18.
[2]Ibid.
[3]Charles Kraft, *Christianity with Power* (Ann Arbor, Mich.: Servant, 1989), p. 112.
[4]Quoted in Johann Christoph Arnold, *Why Forgive?* (Farmington, Penn.: Plough, 2000), p. 44.
[5]Henri Nouwen and Robert Jonas, *Henri Nouwen* (Maryknoll, N.Y.: Orbis, 1998), pp. 39-40.
[6]H. R. Macintosh, *The Christian Experience of Forgiveness* (New York: Harper & Brothers, 1927), p. 192.
[7]David Augsburger, *The Freedom of Forgiveness* (Chicago: Moody Press, 1988), p. 46, emphasis in original.
[8]Leanne Payne, *The Healing Presence* (Westchester, Ill.: Crossway, 1989), p. 89.

Chapter 9: Love Your Enemies

[1]Geoffrey Wainright, *Doxology: The Praise of God in Worship, Doctrine and Life* (New York: Oxford University Press, 1980), p. 434.
[2]"He Never Said a Mumbalin' Word," *The United Methodist Hymnal* (Nashville: United Methodist Publishing House, 1989), p. 291.

[3]I. Howard Marshall, 1 *Peter* (Downers Grove, Ill.: InterVarsity Press, 1991), p. 94.

[4]J. N. D. Kelly, *The Epistles of Peter and Jude* (London: A & C Black, 1969), p. 123.

[5]John Stott, *The Cross of Christ* (Downers Grove, Ill.: InterVarsity Press, 1986), p. 300.

[6]Dan Allender and Tremper Longman III, *Bold Love* (Colorado Springs: NavPress, 1992), p. 187.

[7]Martin Luther King Jr., *Strength to Love* (London: Hodder & Stoughton, 1964), p. 51.

[8]Quoted in David Augsburger, *Helping People Forgive* (Louisville, Ky.: Westminster/John Know, 1996), p. 154.

[9]Stott, *Cross of Christ*, p. 301.

[10]Allender and Longman, *Bold Love*, p. 208.

[11]Ibid., p. 226.

[12]Quoted in C. Hoyt Watson, *DeShazer* (Spring Arbor, Mich.: Saltbox Press, 1991), p. 53.

[13]Ibid., p. 64.

[14]Scott Peck, *People of the Lie* (New York: Simon & Schuster, 1983), pp. 268-69.

Chapter 10: Radiant Scars

[1]Kenneth Woodward, "The Other Jesus," *Newsweek*, March 27, 2000, p. 60.

[2]Quoted in John Stott, *The Cross of Christ* (Downers Grove, Ill.: InterVarsity Press, 1986), p. 21.

[3]Quoted in William Temple, *Reading St. John's Gospel* (London: Macmillan, 1968), p. 366.

[4]Simone Weil, *Gravity and Grace* (London: Routledge & Kegan Paul, 1952), p. 73.

[5]Emil Brunner, *The Christian Doctrine of Creation and Redemption* (Philadelphia: Westminster Press, 1952), p. 181.

[6]Quoted in Paul Barnett, *The Message of 2 Corinthians* (Downers Grove, Ill.: InterVarsity Press, 1988), p. 177.

[7]Don Crossland, *A Journey Toward Wholeness* (Nashville: StarSong Publishing, 1991), p. 101.

[8]Mattie Greathouse, "My Story Is Grounded in Life," *The Asbury Herald* 112, no. 2 and 3 (2000): 8.

[9]Ibid., p. 9.

[10]Ibid.

[11]Ibid.